"In this field-defining, lucidly written book, Leighton Evans draws an authentic, cutting-edge picture of VR experientiality in contrast with other immersive media and opens our eyes to the changes in immersive opportunities afforded by contemporary consumer VR. He presents us with a thoroughly researched genealogy of VR, identifying the specific media-historical moment that has brought about its re-emergence and blending scholarly rigor with refreshing episodes of personal storytelling. The book compellingly embeds its subject matter in the history of digital media more generally, viewed through a sharp, critical lens that reminds us about the commercial dictates under which our hypermediated selves and our technological extensions operate."

—**Astrid Ensslin,** University of Alberta, Canada

The Re-Emergence of Virtual Reality

In this short book, Evans interrogates the implications of VR's re-emergence into the media mainstream, critiquing the notion of a VR revolution by analysing the development and ownership of VR companies while also exploring the possibilities of immersion in VR and the importance of immersion in the interest and ownership of VR enterprises. He assesses how the ideologies and desires of both computer programmers and major Silicon Valley industries may influence how VR worlds are conceived and experienced by users while also exploring the mechanisms that create the immersive experience underpinning interest in the medium.

Leighton Evans is Senior Lecturer in Media Theory at Swansea University, UK. He is the author of *Locative Social Media: Place in the Digital Age* (2015) and co-author of *Location-Based Social Media: Space, Time and Identity* (2017).

Routledge Focus on Digital Culture
Series editor: Andrew Hoskins
University of Glasgow, UK

The digital age has transformed media form and experience. This transformation is best understood as a series of ongoing revolutions: a material revolution in the physical basis, properties and capacities of media; an ecological revolution in the relationships of media form and content and their producers and consumers; a cultural revolution in the economic, political and social organization and operation of society's knowledge and informational experiences; and a personal revolution in the individual's ability to produce and organize their own informational ecology.

This series of short-form books enables timely interventions, critical thinking and analysis of digital revolutions and their histories, and exploration of the entire ecology of digital life.

The Re-Emergence of Virtual Reality
Leighton Evans

The Re-Emergence of Virtual Reality

Leighton Evans

LONDON AND NEW YORK

First published 2019 by Routledge

2 Park Square, Milton Park, Abingdon, Oxfordshire OX14 4RN
52 Vanderbilt Avenue, New York, NY 10017

Routledge is an imprint of the Taylor & Francis Group, an informa business

First issued in paperback 2019

Library of Congress Cataloging-in-Publication Data
A catalog record for this book has been requested

ISBN: 978-1-138-54225-9 (hbk)
ISBN: 978-0-367-42380-3 (pbk)

Typeset in Times New Roman
by Apex CoVantage, LLC

Vielen Dank für deine Geduld! Du bist die Beste. xx

Contents

Figures

Acknowledgements

There are always people who will be missed in acknowledgements, so to those I apologise profusely.

The research underpinning this book was made possible thanks to a research grant through the Rising Stars scheme at the University of Brighton. For their assistance in that successful grant, thanks go to Frauke Behrendt, Anne Galliot and Helen Kennedy. Huge thanks go to Karen Cham who facilitated both the grant and the fieldwork site. At the Digital Catapult, Brighton, my thanks go to Richard Scott, Rosalie Hoskins and the whole team. The research grant allowed me to hire a fantastic research assistant, Darcey Haynes, who deserves many thanks. Also, huge thanks go out also to Lizzy Hallam and Lea Eichinger for helping with the transcription of materials.

Many people helped with the research, putting me in the right direction and making a wealth of helpful suggestions. In no particular order, thanks go out to Pete and Jack Maddalena of VR Craftworks; Sam Watts, director of immersive experiences at Make Real; Simon Wilkinson (CiRCA69); Elise Watson and Ben Kidd of Curiscope; Sophie Dixon and Ed Silverton of Mnemoscene Ltd.; Michael Danks; Jeremiah Ambrose of the University of Brighton; Aoi Nakamura and Esteban Fourmi of aoiesteban.com; Andy Baker of Ixxy; Elvar Sig of Studio Sig and James Turnbull of The Old Market Theatre, Hove, and development manager of #TOMtech (dedication pending). Other incredibly helpful people include Maf'j Alvarez, Danny Goodyale, Mark Grizenko, Ersin han Ersin, Michelle Proksell and many others whom I have probably missed right now. Thanks to all.

At Swansea University, my thanks go to the following colleagues who have either wittingly or unwittingly helped with suggestions and comments while this book was being written: William Merrin, Rhys Jones, Richard Thomas, Mostyn Jones, Yan Wu, Sian Rees, Joanna Rydzewska, Sarah Crowther, Non Vaughan-Williams, Elain Price, Pete Jones, Iwan Williams, Joe Tucker, Neil Woollard, Pete Hanratty and especially Xin Zhao for comments on the first chapter. I've received incredible comments and proofing tips from Liz Wride and Eve Forrest—thank you both. Andy Hoskins deserves a major round of applause for editing the final manuscript so carefully, and Erica Wetter and Emma Sherriff from Routledge both get my thanks.

Final thanks to my parents, who let me waste lots of time as a child playing video games—without that, this would not have happened.

1   Introduction

I've just had a man swing a giant shovel at me trying to decapitate me. After about an hour of creeping around in the dark, feeling my heart beat through my chest. When it happened I screamed because I thought I was going to get hit by this maniac. Thank god nobody was watching me. The headset is covered in sweat. Could be due to the heat, but I'll be honest—I was sweating due to being afraid of the game. That's a genuine first.

These are the notes I made right after my own introduction to a fully integrated virtual reality experience. On the 1 June 2017, I unboxed and began using a PlayStation Virtual Reality (PSVR) headset, and the first experience I had was with *Resident Evil VII*. It was terrifying. Prior to that, a Google Cardboard headset had given me 360° video experiences and games on an iPhone, but this was a huge step up from those mobile virtual reality (VR) experiences. The feeling of an embodied video gaming experience, where I was perceptually linked to the gaze of the game character and every turn of my head was a turn of his head, was new, exciting and petrifying. I'd been playing *Resident Evil* games since 1998, and I've had the 'jump!' effect of being scared by a video game or film countless times. The experience of the game in VR, however, was visceral; previously, I could turn my head, close my eyes, put down the device, or turn off the screen. This time, turning the head did nothing. Closing my eyes meant opening them back up to the same scene. Turning off means an awkward removal of the headset, and the cost of the convenience of taking a breather from the game is too much when using VR. I was stuck *there*.[1] The idea of that *there*, how the *there* is made, how that bears the intentionality of programmers (and power dynamics of the digital economy) and what the possibility of being *there* means for us as users is the impetus for this book.

My reflections on *Resident Evil VII* in the context of this book are more than a mildly amusing anecdote. I had been waiting for that kind of experience for more than 20 years. In the early 1990s, I was a console gaming–obsessed teenager who would devour magazines like *Mean Machines*, *CVG* and *ACE*, which would at irregular intervals tease with the idea that VR was coming. VR was coming very soon, just round the corner and with us when 16-bit machines would be supplanted by 32-bit machines. Or 64-bit. Or 128-bit. Reading interviews with Jaron Lanier on VR and photographs of Virtuality headsets got me excited about the opportunity to exist in a virtual world—and that opportunity never happened. The Nintendo Virtual Boy never came to the UK, having shipped only 770,000 units (Snow, 2007) and ending a buzz around VR in console gaming. The technological buzz of my late teens was around the Internet and surfing the Web rather than VR headsets, and VR passed from popular consciousness. VR had a Hollywood focus in 1995, with *Strange Days*, *Johnny Mnemonic* and *Hackers* following on from the surprise 1992 breakout hit *The Lawnmower Man*, and then just stopped being part of the popular discourse. *eXistenZ* and *The Matrix* in 1999 would add philosophical contours to the story of VR, but despite the interesting existential and metaphysical questions both films raised VR remained quite invisible in popular entertainment. While *The Matrix* was top of the box office in 1999, Lanier's pioneering VR company VPL Research filed for bankruptcy (Virtual Reality Society, 2017). The buzz died, as did visions of living in a VR world in the early 1990s.

Now the buzz is back, and I finally have the opportunity to experience that world that was promised and never delivered in the early 1990s. The re-emergence of VR that this book is concerned with is the re-emergence of the medium in commercial electronics and popular discourse, and the fact that I could have a VR experience like my sweaty, screaming horror at *Resident Evil VII* at home is an indication of a cultural milestone that the medium has passed through in the last few years. In the early 1990s, a commercial VR headset such as VPLs EyePhone headset would have cost around $10,000 (Lanier, 2017: 190). Today, a PSVR retails for under £300, with games. Powerful, PC-based platforms like the Oculus Rift and HTC Vive are catering for the top end of the new market; PSVR and Samsung's Gear represent a mid-range VR market; and Google Cardboard and various other low-cost headsets represent a cheaper, smartphone–powered market. In May 2018, the Oculus Go and Lenovo Mirage Solo arrived, retailing for $199 and $399 respectively, bringing a stand-alone, purely consumer-focused VR headset at commercial-level pricing to the public. VR has arrived.

The development of these commercial VR technologies is enmeshed in the wider digital economy of the 2010s. In 2014, Facebook acquired Oculus VR for $2.3 billion in cash and stock options (Welch, 2014), making VR integrated with the biggest social network in the world. Nvidia (Feltham, 2018) predicts that by 2021, 50 million VR headsets will be sold. By early

2018, Sony had sold more than 2 million PSVR headsets, and while HTC and Oculus have not as yet released sales figures for their Vive and Rift headsets, Google has sold more than 10 million Cardboard headsets (Robertson, 2017) with figures unavailable for the myriad imitators of that kind of VR headset. While the market is currently small, major companies in the digital economy are establishing key positions in the VR market. Facebook own Oculus. Sony have developed a dedicated platform for its PlayStation 4 console. Samsung are developing hardware and a platform. Google are developing hardware, platforms and software for VR. The major digital media companies are staking out their hardware and software platforms as critical services in the emerging commercial market.

With a consumer market for VR, we are seeing a medium that has always promised a revolution in perspective, immersion and mediated experience become available to a mass market for the first time in a technologically suitable form. While *Computer Gaming World* predicted affordable VR by 1994 back in 1992 (Engler, 1992), it has taken another two decades for that prediction of affordability and commercial potential to be realised. However, the world in which the medium is now re-emerging is radically different from the world of the early 1990s. In 1992, the Mosaic Web browser for viewing graphics on the then recently invented World Wide Web had not yet been released; Windows95 was 3 years from release; it would be 12 years before the founding of Facebook. The Internet was a niche communications medium and only available through desktop computing with a dial-up modem. The early promise of VR and the interest in VR in the 1990s, when there appeared a possibility of a commercial breakthrough, were in an entirely different context from the one in which VR is emerging today. Now, billions of people around the world are connected to the Internet via personal media devices and use the Web, social media and other Internet-dependent communications technologies constantly. We are networked individuals, continually connected to the Internet. The idea that we can reside in a cyberspace made possible by a VR headset has been superseded by a reality where we have integrated cyberspace into our everyday lives, a digital media eco-structure dominated by major commercial companies.

This book critically assesses what the re-emergence of commercial VR means in the context of the current digital world, its economics, the environment and the intentions of VR development. As the title of this book suggests, the core question of the book is, "Why is VR re-emerging?" To answer this question, it is necessary to interrogate two other questions. Firstly, the promise of VR as a radical, immersive medium is only now being realised commercially. This book traces an argument that VR withdrew from and re-emerged in consumer media thanks to technological deficiencies but that its re-emergence into a new socio-technical environment questions the very possibility of VR being revolutionary. The critical question to be asked with regard to this is, "How does the emergence of a wider digital culture and economy impact on VR as a re-emerging medium?" As the discourses and imaginaries of VR make much of VR being a revolutionary medium, the dominance of the emerging commercial market in VR by the giants of the digital economy question how revolutionary the re-emergence of VR is (or can be) in practice. Secondly, the possibility of revolutionary immersion itself requires close examination. If this possibility underpins the attraction of VR, then how immersion is achieved and what such immersion could achieve become important considerations. In essence, "What might VR achieve and how in terms of immersion?" By addressing these questions, the intention of this book is to critically assess why VR is re-emerging as a medium and what that means for media users.

Immersion and Virtual Worlds—The Revolutionary Discourse of VR

The choice of the word 'worlds' in the preceding heading is very deliberate, and in this book it will be used to refer to two different but interlocking concepts that are critical in understanding what the re-emergence of VR into the present day world might mean for the development, use and impact of the medium. 'World' refers to the wider social, cultural and technological milieu in which VR is designed, developed and used. 'World,' in a very different sense of the word, also refers to what VR may be able to produce (eventually). Here, I refer to 'world' in a phenomenological sense, as the referential totality of things and other people that make sense to us and that we understand intuitively. This may appear abstract; an illustration, though, is very straightforward. When I find myself in a room with an oven, a stove top, a kettle, knives in a rack, a dishwasher, a fridge and freezer, and I'm wearing rubber gloves and doing the washing up, I know that I am in the kitchen. I don't consciously look around to make this judgement; I know intuitively this is a kitchen based on my experiences of kitchens in the past and of my own kitchen. When I enter a room that I have never been in previously that has these objects, I know I'm in a kitchen. That kitchen might be different from mine in particular ways, but it fits with my concept of kitchen. My kitchen concept is, in a phenomenological context, a 'world'—an existential locale that I know intuitively and without reference to questioning because the referential totality made by the objects in that room 'tell' me it's a kitchen without my questioning. On a day-to-day basis, we pass through these worlds of familiarity countless times without thinking about those places, and our knowing of 'world' in this way is integral to our everyday understanding and functioning.

Digital media devices can be the basis for worlds (see Evans, 2015). Take my experience in *Resident Evil VII*; at first, I was tense and nervous as

I didn't know the game and literally spent the first hour jumping around like a bunny at every shock and scare in the game. After a few hours, I was accustomed to the game. My familiarity with the game meant fewer shocks, fewer scares (albeit some very intense ones still occurred), and my avatar in the game was moving more freely, more quickly and with greater precision than previously. At the same time, I was less consciously aware of the controller in my hand, more confident and less reflective with button presses and handling the controller. My familiarity had brought a feeling of world-hood; the tools I was using passed away from circumspection, and I was familiar with the game environment. Regular gamers will be all too familiar with this feeling, that the controller fades away, and we are completely comfortable in that world of the game, as will those of us who use a keyboard to type regularly or a smartphone to access social networking. The device fades away as it is part of the experience of the 'world' we are in.

The potential of VR as a medium—and this was the potential that excited people back in the 1980s and 1990s as well as today—is that this kind of worldhood, or feeling of world, can be made in a medium that is far more immersive than my video game console broadcast through an LED TV. A VR headset provides an enclosed visual field for the user; headphones cancel out the sound of the outside world; haptic devices can provide sensory feedback loops of touch, pain, heat or cold.[2] While immersion is a feature of many kinds of effective media—I feel immersed in a good novel, at a compelling play, in the cinema with a good film or in my video game—the potential and promise of VR were to intensify, perfect and idealise immersion because of the sensory affordances of the medium. The potential to build worlds, or the potential for a feeling of worldhood, in VR is critical when considering the potential of VR as a consumer medium. Being immersed in a VR world might just be the most intense media experience we can have—but the worlds built in VR are contextualised and shaped by the world in which VR is emerging. VR applications, systems, platforms and hardware are the products of design principles and organisations that have ideological and political character that will shape the form of the VR worlds being made. So, world in this book has a dual articulation or meaning. The emergence of consumer VR demands that we pay attention to how worlds can be made in VR and to how the wider world or context in which VR develops shapes and affects the VR worlds that we are now being encouraged to experience and inhabit.[3]

Whatever Happened to the VR Revolution 1.0?

I have already referred to the excitement around VR that was a feature of near and distant visions of computing in the early 1990s. Understanding why that excitement did not deliver on the vision of the technology is important in giving context to the current new wave of VR. Lister et al. (2009: 106–107) provided some pertinent thoughts on this when discussing their own comments on VR from an earlier edition of their own book on new media. They state that VR, as a medium, once had a discourse surrounding it that was every bit as absorbing and hyped as the Internet but that did not deliver on that hype and expectation like the Internet and the World Wide Web would so spectacularly from the mid-1990s. The authors note that "the enthusiasm for VR was part of the euphoric techno-utopian expectations of the period, and the heady mix of the computer counter-culture and neo-liberal Silicon Valley entrepreneurship—a period that was brought to a fairly abrupt end by the dotcom bust of 2000" (2009: 106). The zeitgeist of the 1980s and 1990s computational and digital development will be discussed in Chapter 2 on the history of VR but it is worth unpicking some of the points that Lister et al. make here to set the context for this book. The dotcom bust of 2000 may well have played a role in the decrease in commercial interest in VR, as VR was a capital-intensive technology that had (despite more than a decade and a half of hype and investment) yet to make a major inroad into the commercial electronics market.

Of more importance, though, is an additional point made by Lister et al. through a quote from Stephen Ellis, lead researcher in the Advanced Displays and Spatial Perception Lab at NASA, who stated that "the technology of the 1980s was not mature enough" (Lister et al., 2009: 106). The early period of VR was characterised by a vision that was far ahead of the technological possibilities of the time. In the late 2010s, the technology has begun (but not yet reached or surpassed) the vision of VR from the 1980s. This lack of fit, which will be referred to as a 'technological lag' in this book, is far more salient in the delay in the emergence of VR in the commercial electronics and entertainment space. Technological lag is a referent to cultural lag (Woodard, 1934: 388), the phenomenon that culture takes time to catch up with technological innovations and that social problems and conflicts are caused by this lag. With technological lag, technology has had to catch up with the vision of the medium, causing a gap between the idealism of the original wave of VR and the realities and structures of the digital economy in the present day. The 'euphoric techno-utopianism' of the 1980s and 1990s required technological developments that afforded (Gibson, [1979] 2015) the possibility of realising those visions. While those technological affordances are either now with us or on the way, the contention in this book is that the vision itself may have been swamped by the heady mix of the computer counterculture and neo-liberal Silicon Valley entrepreneurship, or Californian Ideology (Barbrook and Cameron, 1996). The possibility of a cyberspace where people can interact, experience new approaches to sensation, perception and embodiment and have a radically different *world* from the everyday world contrasts with technologies dominated by companies whose primary business model is the production, aggregation and selling of personal data for profit.

That euphoric techno-utopianism of the discourses around 1990s VR was a reflection of the implicit and explicit revolutionary nature of VR as radically immersive and intimate. However, the revolutionary nature of VR as a medium in itself is questionable. The VR revolution and the potential of VR to be a new medium were predicated on the possibility of being in another world. Sirius (2007) described that notion as:

> These 3D worlds would be accessed through head-mounted displays. The idea was to put the user literally *inside* computer-created worlds, where she could move around and see and hear the goings on in a fully dimensional alternative reality and have the sensation of being in another world. The eyes were the primary organs of entrance into these other worlds, although touch, motion and sound were all also involved.[4]

This is still the potential of VR today, and in this potential the claims of a revolutionary medium lie—a fully alternative, computer-generated reality that we can be fully immersed within. However, the presence of major digital media companies in the VR space, producing platforms, application and hardware, suggests that the potential for a revolutionary form of immersive experience needs to be considered in the context of digital media economics, politics, social attitudes and ideologies. Therefore, this book critiques the notion of a VR revolution by analysing the development and ownership of VR companies while also exploring the possibilities of immersion in VR and the importance of immersion in the interest and ownership of VR enterprises. This book will build an argument that explores critically why these major developers and companies want to dominate a media form that *builds computer-generated worlds that are intended for people to dwell in.* The promise of immersion and a revolutionary media experience is intimately linked to the aims, objectives and ideologies of the companies that are seeking to dominate the VR hardware, software and platform markets. This argument therefore critically assesses how the ideologies and desires of both computer programmers and major Silicon Valley industries currently influence, and will influence in the future, how these worlds are conceived and experienced by users while also exploring the mechanisms that create the immersive experience that underpins interest in the medium.

This is the inaugural book in the Routledge *Focus on Digital Culture* series, and VR is a digital medium that needs to be understood in that context of digital culture. The development of VR since the 1960s did not take place in a vacuum from the rest of computational technology or digital cultures; VR develops as part of a wider technological and cultural frame, and VR as a medium reflects, embodies and problematizes cultural issues. Palmer Luckey invented the Oculus Rift, but he's also a prominent Donald Trump supporter known for his funding of 'shitposting'[5] during the 2016 American Presidential Election. The development of Oculus did not occur outside of this political inclination; while Luckey might be an extreme case and not indicative of the politics of Silicon Valley, the intentionality and politics of designers, programmers and manufacturers should be thought of as written large into the design, materiality and experience of VR. The politics, economics and social relations of the communities that make VR effect the possibility of there being a revolutionary nature to VR: will we be receiving new worlds, or will we be harvested for data and subjected to fake news, political messages and controlled platforms inscribed with ideologies and intentions beyond our control? In a highly immersive medium that (in an ideal situation) has control over the senses and sensory information flows, this is a pertinent question about the re-emergence of VR.

What Is VR?

'VR' as a term has been around much longer than one might think. In 1938, Antonin Artaud (1958) explained the illusory nature of characters and objects in the theatre as "la réalité virtuelle"; the English translation of this in 1958 is the earliest published use of the term 'virtual reality'. Definitions of VR have been numerous since the 1980s' emergence of scholarly and popular interest in VR. Jaron Lanier (2017) offers no fewer than 52 different definitions of VR spanning a number of uses and contexts of VR. Lanier offers definitions that draw out the importance of cognition, perception, dreaming, existentialism and phenomenology in that VR emphasises the actuality of existing consciously, empathy and hallucinating. Less ambitiously, VR has been defined as providing "a more intimate interface between humans and computer imagery" (Woolley, 1992: 5); a system that gives the user an experience of being 'immersed' in a synthesised environment (Earnshaw, Gigante, and Jones, 1994: iv); and immersion in virtual worlds and interaction with objects informing those worlds, giving the feeling that the person is a real participant in the virtual world (Magnenat-Thalmann and Thalmann, 1994: xi). Negroponte (1995: 117) describes VR simply as 'being there' with the 'there' being a computer-generated simulation. Hillis (1999: xiv) defines VR as a technological reproduction of the process of perceiving the real. Sherman and Craig (2002: 6–10) describe VR as being inclusive of four elements: a virtual world, immersion, sensory feedback and interactivity. McMenemy and Ferguson (2007: 4) suggest "a computer-generated 3D environment within which users can participate in real time and experience a sensation of 'being there'".

These definitions are just some of the many that have been offered for VR over the past two and a half decades. All are similar, albeit stressing different aspects of VR in the various definitions. It is interesting to note some of the verbs used in the definitions: immersed, interaction, feeling, being, perceiving, participate. The use of these verbs stress that any definition of VR includes some kind of activity and that VR is therefore not a passive media form. VR is an active medium, and the user is the key in that activity rather than the content of the VR environment being experienced. As Jerald (2009) stresses, a VR system consists of a series of inputs from the user within an application that are rendered by the hardware of the system in order to produce an output that is experienced by the user as a virtual experience. The inputs of the user in a VR environment are a constitutive part of the VR environment. So, the medium of VR is not the one that shows a 360° video on a head-mounted display (HMD), a frequently used term for a VR headset, where the user is being shown a video with no interactivity. This argument would state that the necessary aspects of a VR environment are interactivity and participation in the environment on the part of the user—which is not possible as an observer in a 360° video. I return to why this is problematic at the end of this chapter.

While including these aspects of user interaction in VR in a definition is important, other mediums can include these elements of interactivity and immersion. It is important to delineate what VR *is not* as much as it is to establish what it is. I labour over this point because, currently, there is a considerable conflation of VR with other kinds of computer-mediated realities, specifically augmented reality (AR) and mixed reality (MR), both of which can incorporate immersion and interactivity. Indeed, these two computer-mediated realities could be seen as conflated; Lanier (2017: 202) argues that MR and AR are the same as each other and that the difference between them is simply a matter of platform rather than formal difference. Milgram and Kishino (1994) argue that reality itself can take a number of forms and therefore can be considered through a range of different reality states on a virtuality continuum from the real environment to the virtual. VR and AR are on that continuum, with MR being a point on the continuum that can be broken down into AR and augmented virtuality (AV). This virtuality continuum moves from the real environment (the 'real' world that we live in, which is in itself interpreted subjectively by us as human beings), to AR (adding cues or digital objects over the existing real world via a digital interface), to AV (capturing real world content and bringing that into VR), and to virtual environments (artificially or computationally created environments made without capturing any content from the real world) (Jerald, 2015: 29–30).

While this model differentiates AR and VR in a sensible way, the differentiation of VR and virtual environments adds a layer of complexity to what VR is as a medium. As Jerald (2015: 30) explains, a virtual environment is artificially created without input from the physical world that achieves the goal of engaging a user in an experience so that she feels presence in that world. Reality or the real environment is forgotten in such an experiential state. Such a virtual environment may be seen as an ideal form or state of VR, where the goal of complete immersion has been realised. Whether this state can be realised will be a function not only of the environment designed (with regard to the sensory stimulation it provides and the type and character of environment) but also the orientation of the user towards that experience. It can be argued that many designers of VR are not trying to make a virtual environment in this sense. The use of physical props and environments as primers and environmental stabilisers for VR is well established,[6] for example. Also, while VR designers may not incorporate material from real environments, VR designs may well be closely based upon or aim to recreate accurately real environments. The understanding of the user of a VR environment will nearly always be in comparison to a real environment too, so the bracketing off of real environments—even when deeply immersed in VR—will be difficult as it is the experience of real environments that will underpin the experience of VR. Therefore, while as a theoretical category virtual environments provide a useful endpoint to the continuum of reality experiences that differentiate the real, AR and VR, in practice these environments may be difficult to achieve or undesirable for VR creators.

So VR is often not a full virtual environment in the way that Jerald (2015: 30) suggests, as the applications and experiences that people use with commercial VR platforms will often be modelled on or will borrow substantially from the real environment. However, there can be fully virtual environments that do not borrow from the real environment in any way. Playing a game like *Polybius* in VR, where shooting gameplay is blended with inconsistent and vivid geometrical environments, you could not imagine a similar real experience. In constructing a consensual definition of VR where the term refers to computer-generated experiential environments where users can interact with the environment with the aim of immersing them to the extent that they feel that they are 'being there', the virtual environment and environments including, influenced by or mimicking the real environment can all be considered VR. Within this definition of VR, the activity and orientation of the user towards the VR experience are brought into close focus. Additionally, such an approach conceptualizes VR as a number of different kinds or techniques of mediation that combine to create the effect of the experience of a computer-mediated reality as identified by Heim (1998): simulation, interaction, artificiality, immersion, telepresence, full-body immersion and networked communications. This kind of definition lends itself towards a concept of VR as an assemblage of different immersive elements, and Chapter 4 of this book will develop this approach to understanding what immersion in VR is with reference to interviews with professionals from the VR industry.

All the definitions discussed here characterise VR as a revolutionary medium with the potential for radical immersive experiences through sensory stimulation and offering new ways of interacting with the objects and things in a virtual world. On the latter point, it can be argued that there is some way to go in consumer VR. While the HTC Vive, Oculus Rift and PSVR offer controllers that allow for the manipulation of objects and things in interacting with the VR environment presented, these are still limited by the lack of dedicated haptic input devices. However, these platforms now exist in a commercial environment, and these can be seen as genuine VR platforms in the way that a 360° video experienced on a smartphone in a cardboard headset is not. If one excludes the possibility that empathy, fear, happiness or joy (or any other emotion) is not interaction with a medium, then much of the research and theory on television or cinema audiences would be rendered obsolete. Considering the re-emergence of VR requires a close examination of the technology and platforms and, importantly, users of the medium—as the preceding definitions emphasise over and over again, both the technology and the user are co-constitutive of VR experiences. So, 360° video may not technologically or ontologically be VR, a feeling of immersion experienced by people viewing 360° video in an HMD questions this delineation of VR types. The 360° video experience characterises many of the early attempts at VR experiences by cinema distributors, sporting organisations and media distributors and can be experienced on a VR headset as well as on a cardboard HMD. As these experiences are both marketed as VR to users and often experienced as VR by users and as this book concerns the re-emergence of VR as a commercial concern, these experiences can be considered while keeping the differentiation between 360° and VR if one positions 360° on Jerald's (2015) reality continuum beyond AR but not fully VR.

Revolution or Control—The Re-Emergence of Consumer VR

Given the preceding definitions, it is safe to say that VR is considered a medium that offers something—immersion, interaction, even co-presence— that other media cannot due to the degree of intimacy and interaction that VR can achieve. The revolutionary nature of the medium, then, is taken as a given in how VR is defined. However, in closely examining the re-emergence of VR, this revolutionary nature may be questioned. In approaching three key questions that arise from the re-emergence of VR—what happened to VR and why is it re-emerging; what may VR deliver as a medium; and how the emergence of a wider digital culture and economy impacts on VR as a re-emerging medium—there is, at the core of this book, a critical questioning of how this revolutionary image of the medium contrasts with the political economy, mechanisms of control and ubiquity of many of the companies now involved heavily in the re-emergence of the medium. Additionally, questions arise of just how revolutionary a VR experience is with regards to immersion. Immersion as a property should not be taken as a given just by having a HMD on a head. How one becomes immersed in VR is an important question, especially as the hardware, platforms and software that a VR experience are dependent upon will be linked to major organisations in the digital economy that have their own needs with regard to data accumulation, advertising, ideology and control. The main argument of this book is that, while the promise of VR as an immersive medium with scope for immersion beyond other media is a revolutionary one in terms of how media users stand in relation to media content, the politics and economics of VR follow many current debates within digital media that should call into question the revolutionary nature of the medium.

So, with regard to the question of how the emergence of a wider digital culture and economy has impacted on VR as a medium, a discussion of the cultural history of VR (that is, what has shaped VR as a medium over the course of its development) is married to an analysis of the major organisations involved in the return of VR (Google, Sony, Facebook, Samsung, HTC), who are investing vast sums into the development of the medium, is necessary. Engaging with this aspect of the re-emergence of VR involves interrogation of the political economy of consumer VR and an analysis of the production of VR as a commercial medium and the relation of that production to power in the digital economy. To consider what might VR achieve and how in terms of immersion involves an analysis of the design practices of VR. To do this, I interviewed 21 VR designers, programmers, innovators and researchers to understand how VR experiences are produced, what the relationships between design and the market tell us about how VR is being shaped for the consumer market and how VR experiences are made. These opinions and insights are analysed through an examination of the possibility of immersion and worldhood. Essentially, that question is answered by analysing what immersion is, how immersive experiences are made and what the principles of immersion are in themselves.

To answer these questions, Chapter 2 sets out a brief cultural history of VR to assess how different aspects of wider academic, political and social cultural epochs have affected the development of VR over time and have contributed to why the medium is re-emerging now. Any history of VR rejects a naïve notion that VR re-emerged as a bolt from the blue in 2010 after a gap from the 1990s. This chapter considers a series of 'histories' of VR that converge to offer an understanding of the kind of consumer medium that is currently re-emerging: antecedents of VR from the Victorian era that indicate the potential of immersive experience and show the initial experimentations in the perceptual and psychological aspects of current-day VR; the emergence of the first VR headsets in the 1950s and early 1960s as a counterbalance to cybernetics and the dominance of computer interfaces in the human–computer relationship; a cultural studies history of postmodern and post-structural thinking on the virtual and the real that contextualises the virtual in modern culture; the 1980s as a time of idealism in VR as a reaction to contemporary computing, which stood in contrast to VR imaginaries in science fiction and popular culture as dystopian; and the 1990s and 2000s as a critical 'dark history' where significant advancements were made (away from the spotlight of popular culture) that overcame the technological lag that defeated early 1990s VR but that also paved the way for the re-emerging consumer VR today that is a battleground between immersive revolution and commercial control.

Continuing to reflect on how the emergence of a wider digital culture and economy impacts on VR as a re-emerging medium, Chapter 3 adopts a political economy approach to lay the groundwork for how the digital economy has affected, does affect and will continue to affect the development of VR. The 'new wave' of VR has seen major investment in infrastructure and hardware from many of the biggest companies in the digital economy. The presence of such large digital players in the field heavily suggests that they see VR as a major market, but their different approaches also illustrate a number of different trajectories that commercial VR may take over the medium term. The business decisions to invest in VR by the various companies are reflections of their positions and ambitions in the digital economy; thus the near-future and potential impact of VR can be assessed through a close inspection of the practices of these major organisations.

Chapter 4 moves the focus to the second question of what might VR achieve and how in terms of immersion. To understand immersion in VR, interviews with 21 VR developers, programmers and artists were conducted to understand how immersion is created and made, as well as the key elements as seen by VR makers in creating an immersive experience in VR. This analysis of immersion poses questions about the radical nature of VR as an immersive medium, given that the elements of immersion identified (vision, audio, touch, narrative and mood or orientation) are not exclusive to VR but are all part of immersion in other mediums too. What emerged from these interviews is that immersion is an assemblage of these elements rather than an emergent property of simply having VR equipment and that the maintenance of fidelity continua or consistency in experience is the critical factor in establishing, building and maintaining immersion in VR. VR is also still waiting for the kind of interface that might facilitate full, deep immersion of the kind that discourses on immersion in VR would have us believe is a property of the medium. For commercial VR, there is still some way to go.

Consumer VR is here, just not normally distributed yet. Chapter 5 follows on from Chapter 4 by looking at what barriers to widespread VR adoption still exist and how these might be overcome. Based again on the research with VR professionals, a number of barriers to uptake were identified—some with solutions, others without. Issues considered include that VR is dependent upon expensive material devices as well as global communications networks; that the use of VR is currently restrained by its material base; that VR makes many people sick—the nausea issue; that VR is very expensive; and that, as yet, there is no language that allows programmers and developers to discuss VR coherently with customers and the consumer.

Chapter 6 contextualises the historical, economic, ideological and metaphysical arguments already made in this book through examples of how VR is currently making a cultural impact—what VR we are being offered as consumers. This chapter focuses on some of the most popular current uses of VR: video games, social networking, and pornography. The affordances of the VR medium allow for a reconceptualisation and re-mediation of each of these media forms, and this in turn results in a change in the subject position of the audience (possibly towards more *empathy*) and a transformation of what it means to be an audience member when experiencing media in VR. Recall though that the definitions of VR emphasise a revolutionary aspect to the medium; VR can give more intense immersive experiences of these media texts than if they were experienced in other mediums. Given the ownership, the practices of making VR and the immersion assemblage as conditioning factors in the effectiveness of VR, this chapter questions the current value of VR in these genres and media types and therefore addresses both key questions.

The final chapter offers a summary of the current state of VR and what that means for the future of VR *in the short term* with regard to how VR is portrayed in fiction in 2018. What VR needs in order to move from a marginal media interest to a position of revolutionary dominance is contingent on how the vision of VR as providing a metaverse for human existence can be achieved. The possibility of this vision, inspired by films like *Ready Player One*, is considered in this chapter in light of the findings of this book as a whole.

Notes

1. Stuck there with 400,000 other players or 13.05% of players of *Resident Evil VII* on the PlayStation 4 according to the company who made the game Capcom (2018).
2. This technology has been available for a long time; Thomas Zimmerman developed the original DataGlove for VPL, which was brought to market in 1987 (Foley, 1987).
3. In January 2018, Google and Lenovo launched the Mirage Solo headset with Google's own tracking system utilising Inside-out tracking, called 'WorldSense'. This tracking system, using a combination of built-in cameras and a set of sensors, accurately tracks its and therefore the wearer's head position in 3D space (Torres, 2018). Although I'm certain Google was not referring to a phenomenological view of world when naming this system, the fact that making sense of the world is in the name of the system is interesting.
4. Also cited in Lister et al. (2009: 106).
5. The Urban Dictionary (n.d) defines 'shitposting' as the "constant posting of mildly amusing but usually unfunny memes, videos or other pictures that are completely random or unrelated to any discussions". Hern (2016) detailed that Luckey was a secret backer of a group (Nimble America) dedicated to Donald Trump support through 'meme magic' over social media and had posted about this on the notorious Reddit subreddit r/TheDonald as NimbleRichMan.
6. For example, see the Habitats VR exhibition by Marshmallow Laser Feast including *In The Eyes of the Animal* that uses flora and other material in sculpted headsets to create a 'forest' perceptual set (Walton, 2016).

2   A (Brief) Cultural History of VR

The intention of this chapter is not to give a complete and comprehensive history of VR. Writing such a history is beyond the scope of this book and has already been done elsewhere (see Harris, 2018; Lanier, 2017). Instead of repeating and reinterpreting the histories covered in those books, this chapter aims to outline a historical account of the cultural moments that are important in the development of VR. The history of VR here is a history of cultural frames of VR that provide a roadmap to the 2010s re-emergence of VR as a cultural phenomenon. An exploration of the image culture of the mid- to late Victorian age gives historical context not only to the possibility of an immersive sensory medium but also historicises the identification and refinement of perceptual techniques in immersive media that are further developed in VR. A discussion of the first steps in what is identifiably modern VR in the late 1950s contextualises VR within the frame of cybernetic theory and questions why VR was developed in light of the visions of human–computer relationships at the time. A cultural studies history of the dominance of visual culture identifies the virtualisation of reality in the late 20th and early 21st century that provides an opening for VR as a consumer medium. The history of the first wave of VR in the 1980s and 1990s illustrates a conceptual gap between the imaginary of VR and the actuality of VR at the time, as well as how this gap led to the long wait for commercial computing to catch up with the vision of VR. Each history is a step towards the re-emergence of VR, which is as cultural as it is technological.

Georgian and Victorian VR: Panoramas, Stereoscopic Images and Kinetoscopes

For a cultural history of VR, an appropriate starting point would be a cultural moment where some of the principles of VR became part of the cultural zeitgeist at that time. As MacLeod and Moser (1996: xvii) argue, VR should be understood as part of a continuum of technological developments, and in tracing those developments, an appropriate place to begin is in Georgian (George III and George IV of Britain) and Victorian urban amusements. Take, for example, the development and popularity of the panorama. The panorama was a Georgian public amusement invented by Robert Baker in 1787. The original panorama was a sketching of Edinburgh from Calton Hill in the centre of the city that attempted to create a 360° view from that point (Oettermann, 1997: 99). This was not just a painting but an entire technical ensemble involving a fake viewing platform, the limits of the painting being obscured to create an illusory effect of the boundaries of the field of vision, real objects and terrain effects and lighting based on overhead effects and natural light (Oettermann, 1997: 101). The aim of this was immersion: to produce a completely enclosed perception and a full reality effect using deception of all the senses. This fidelity would, ideally, emerge as the distinction between the real and the panorama disappeared. Barker opened this panorama in Edinburgh in 1788 and displayed it in London in 1789. The success of this led to the opening of a rotunda in Leicester Square in 1793 with his son, Henry Aston Barker (Oettermann, 1997: 108). This rotunda was another major technological assemblage needed to support the illusion of the panorama and was also a socio-technical assemblage of businessmen, financiers, architects, designers, teams of workers, project coordinators and artists (Comment, 2003: 18). These shows in London became a success, with a visit from the Royal Family in 1794 of a panorama of the British naval fleet showing the appeal of this form in high society.

While the panorama would decline through the 18th century as other mediums emerged, the aim of the panorama to produce a form of total reality by erasing the real in favour of itself (a form of 'hyperrealism')—albeit the claim of immersion by the panorama is questionable. One can instantly see the link here to VR, a medium that (in some definitions) looks to replace reality with a computer-generated reality. While the panorama has an artistic basis, its importance is in the realm of technical media simulation of reality, which is the same phenomena being attempted using VR. Oettermann (1997: 127) notes that the panorama was the symbolic form of the bourgeoisie, in that the panorama represented its vision of nature and the world. This vision was a limitless perspective, a grasping of the whole and control of the world. This political vision is best expressed in Debord's *Society of the Spectacle*: "In societies where modern conditions of production prevail, all of life presents itself as an immense accumulation of spectacles" (Debord, 1977: 1). The industrial logic of society in the late 18th and early 19th centuries led to the development of media that captured natural phenomena as an artificial spectacle, as a simulation of reality in VR would.

During the Victorian age, a number of technological and commercial improvements on the panorama allowed for a personal, rather than public, experience of immersive media. The development of stereoscopic images by Sir Charles Wheatstone in 1838 foregrounds current VR trends. Stereoscopic images create the illusion of three-dimensional depth from two-dimensional images through the presentation of a slightly different image to each eye, with the eye itself adjusting to this asymmetry by adding depth to the perceived image. Wheatstone's original stereoscope used a pair of mirrors at 45° angles to the user's eyes, each reflecting a picture located off to the side. As this viewer predated many photographic technologies, the pictures used were often drawn, wire-frame images of the kind that would be recreated in VR systems more than a century later (Welling, 1987: 23). Sir David Brewster invented Brewster's Stereoscope in 1849, a handheld viewing device that used the principles of stereoscopy to bring depth to photographs placed in the viewer (Gilbert, 1980: 137). (See Figure 2.1.) This was the first portable 3D viewing device, and the principles underpinning that device are the same as the use of a smartphone with a Google Cardboard or similar device today. Oliver Wendell Holmes and Joseph Bates improved this design in 1861 and patented the Holmes-Bates viewer, which became a fixture in Victorian homes (Gilbert, 1980: 133). This invention

Figure 2.1 Brewster's Stereoscope

(Source: "Brewster's Stereoscope, 1870," Alessandro Nassari, Museo Nazionale della Scienza e della Tecnologia Leonardo da Vinci, Milano, 2014, www.museoscienza.org/dipartimenti/ catalogo_collezioni/images/06055_dia.jpg)

created a new class of photographer, the stereographer, whose role was to create images for stereoscopic cards to sate the demands of a vast new market (Gilbert, 1980: 134). For the purposes of cultural history, Batchen (1998: 276) argues that the stereoscope parallels the experience of VR and therefore questions the notion that VR is revolutionary or new, as it is in fact rooted in the techniques of stereoscopy from more than 150 years ago. The popularity of the stereoscope also foregrounds VR as a commercial medium; there has clearly been a market and demand for the kind of visual experience that VR provides.

At the end of the Victorian era, the development of early cinema technologies saw technical and ergonomic factors that can be seen in VR today. Thomas Edison's Kinetoscope (Nasaw, 1999: 132), a single-person viewer or a strip of backlit film through a peephole, was a precursor of the solitary, spatially confined viewing experience that the mounting of a HMD for VR provides today. Before projection changed the fledgling medium of cinema, the Kinetoscope provided a cheap and popular public amusement, with parlours and multiple machines proving popular at the end of the 19th Century. Although Edison's invention would be superseded quickly after its invention in 1892, its importance here is, like the panorama and stereoscope, in the historical lineage to VR that the technology provides. The dominance of a field of view and the use of moving imagery in the Kinetoscope are obvious features of the VR experience today. The rich visual culture of the Georgian and Victorian age illustrates a public demand and market for the kind of novel and immersive experiences that VR can deliver (albeit in a more technically sophisticated manner). Indeed, the attempts of these earlier media to aim for a fidelity effect that erased the barrier between the real and the simulated in these media is much the same as the aim of VR today. The success of these media as early forms of visual mass media illustrates a cultural demand for immersive media (although claiming full immersion would be optimistic for any of these media forms) and a set of techniques that would be mimicked in VR—albeit at a greater level of sophistication thanks to the computational technologies on which current-day VR systems are dependent.

Cybernetics, Human–Computer Interaction and the Sword of Damocles

The role of computation in VR is obviously something that sets aside the modern-day headset from the panorama or Kinetoscope. The need for computation in combining a rich visual environment of movement with audio, haptic interfaces and the ability to 'move' as an avatar in VR are all obvious differences between VR and the mediums just discussed. The early culture of computation, particularly in an academic context, is also a critical factor in the first instance of VR as a technology. This culture was cybernetics, which as a theoretical discipline is concerned with control and communications in both animal and machine. The emergence of the earliest VR headsets can be seen both within the cybernetic culture and as a response to some of the more dehumanising aspects of cybernetic theory as a way of realigning the relationship between humans and computers.

Cybernetics developed as mathematicians, scientists and engineers struggled with the problems of designing and implementing accurate communication and anti-aircraft systems during World War II (Lister et al., 2003: 353). Following success in improving such systems during World War II, cybernetics emerged as an approach to understanding not only machine communication but also human communication. Norbert Wiener, a critical figure in the history of cybernetics and computer science, defined cybernetics as the scientific study of control and communication in the animal and the machine (Wiener, [1948] 2016). The development of sophisticated control and communication techniques for machines, computational techniques that allowed for the execution of real-time adjustments in telemetry of missile guiding systems, were therefore applied not only to machines but also to humans.

Cybernetics is most visible in the humanities with reference to communication. While cybernetics developed hand in hand with the increasing sophistication and use of computers and computing in communications and systems control, the theory was also applied to human communications. The best known application of cybernetics in media theory is Claude Shannon and Warren Weaver's model of communication ([1948] 1999). The model proposes that the communication process (including human communication) can be understood as a linear process where a signal is sent from a sender to a receiver via a transmission that passes through a particular channel to be received. The fundamental problem of communication in such a model is for the receiver to be able to identify what data came from the sender based on the signal it receives through the channel, therefore avoiding information entropy (Shannon, 1948: 379). The key to communication of this type is that any signal should be able to produce a response—the idea that a message is to be *understood* is not important. It is this that is the root of controversy about information theory and early cybernetics in general; the notion of communication is reduced to response only. John Fiske (1990: 6–7) goes further and argues that this is a model not of communication but of propaganda. The controversy therefore is in the notion of a lack of interpretation on the part of the receiver and hence providing a misrepresentation of human communication due to the simplicity of the model and the inability to consider the context of communication (Chandler, 1994).

Less attention is paid to the more contentious element of control in cybernetics. Arguably, this is more important than the issues of the application of the theory to communication. Consider Norbert Wiener's seminal text on cybernetics, *The Human Use of Human Beings.*

Wiener (1954: 61) argues that feedback loops and mechanisms are a method of controlling a system by reinserting the results of past performance. Any information that results in a change to a process or a method of action can be called learning. Cybernetics therefore becomes the theory of messages (Wiener, 1954: 77) or the organisation of messages (1954: 95) rather than being concerned with the messages themselves or any interpretation of the message, much as in Shannon and Weaver's model. The phenomenology of message reception and understanding is cast aside as mere ephemera; the message, the processing of the message and the action resulting from that processing are all that is important. Moreover, control through systems becomes a function of the nature of the success of the signal of control rather than of the moral or ethical dimension of the communication itself. Lanier (2017: 57) interprets that, in this cybernetic system, humans can be understood only as part of a system with computers, not outside of that system or using computers to achieve ends only on the basis of being human. Lanier describes this vision as terrifying, a precursor to a kind of zombie apocalypse (2017: 58) where humans respond to messages they do not interpret and understand.

This critique has much further to travel. N. Katherine Hayles argues that cybernetics reduces human identity itself to an information pattern rather than an embodied aspect of being human. Through cybernetics (or in a cybernetic position), information has "lost its body" (Hayles, 2010: 2), and information has become disembodied in the work of Wiener and Shannon. A logical conclusion to this is that cybernetics annihilates the rational subject (Hayles, 2010: 110), as humans and machine now exist in the same category. Hayles's counterargument to the cybernetic view of human–computer interaction is that the human is always embodied in a way that the computer is not and that embodiment means intelligence will unfold differently than machine intelligence will (Hayles, 2010: 248). We read 'in the body' for example, a subvocal and physical action that is not the same as the pattern recognition of a machine 'reading'. In an early cybernetic view of the human, we are simple signal makers and responders—zombies of the computer age.

These insights were fortunately not lost on contemporaries of the early cybernetic theorists. Lanier (2017: 57) argues that the term 'artificial intelligence'[1] (AI) was coined to differentiate emerging computer science from Wiener's vision as the vision of this discipline in Wiener's work was deeply troubling. AI understands computers without reference to humans;

cybernetics (at least in the form Wiener propitiated) understands both humans and computers only in reference to one another. As AI moved away from the original cybernetic vision of human–computer interactions, other computer scientists were developing the first computational steps in VR. J.C.R. Licklider (1960) outlined the need for a simpler concept of how humans would interact with computers, delineating the tasks that man and machine would perform in the computer age. While early cybernetics saw man and machine as part of the same system, with communication, response and feedback loops negating any semantic aspect of communication, Licklider foresaw interfaces such as graphical computing and point-and-click interfaces akin to those we are familiar and comfortable with today. In 1963, Ivan Sutherland would formulate the principles of the WIMP (windows, icon, mouse, pointer) environment, which has become the foundation and enduring mode of communication with and through computers to the present day, in a PhD thesis supervised by Claude Shannon (Sutherland, 1963). Sutherland's thesis is also credited with the invention of computer graphics (Lanier, 2017: 42). The work of Licklider and Sutherland indicates a desire to reposition human–computer interaction away from the brutalism of the early cybernetic systems designs to interfaces where computer outputs would take a symbolic form that was meaningful for the user. The externalisation of the vast array of signals and electrical activity in the computer into a form that could be displayed on a screen visually removed the notion of human–computer interaction as a system of signals and responses only— now, the workings of the computer could be seen.

However, even in this major paradigm shift, the way that that signal could be seen is still open to question. The projection of computer signals onto a screen through the process of translation of the electrical signals into meaningful signs would become the dominant form of interface as we well know. However, this was not the only form that symbolic interaction could have taken at the same time that early VR projects emerge—and VR can easily be thought of as an alternative mode of interfacing with computers in a symbolic form. Other media innovators were making steps towards the material form of VR in the late 1950s. Mort Heilig would develop what Jaron Lanier considers the first HMDs in the form of Sensorama arcade machines that would eventually appear to a commercial audience in 1962. The machine itself was simple—a stereo movie played in a headset rather than projected onto a screen—but the headset also incorporated other stimuli such as shaking the body and blowing air to mimic wind (Lanier, 2017: 43).

In 1965, Sutherland began working on a display headset for computers that would allow for the cybernetic feedback loop between man and machine to take a graphical and tactile form (Lister et al., 2003: 112). Sutherland's work was influenced by the flight simulators of the 1960s, which mimicked the physical movements and inputs of flight control without having a cor-responding visual input for trainee pilots. In 1968, Sutherland built an HMD to "present the user with a perspective image which changes as he moves" (Sutherland, 1968: 757). The image that the user saw within the headset was a computer-generated grid (a Cartesian grid that was not unlike the wire-frame drawings of Wheatstone's original stereoscope) that regenerated and changed in line with movements on the part of the user, and this image was presented stereoscopically to provide depth cues for the user to interpret the environment as 3D. Sutherland did not envisage the headset as being lim-ited to just flight simulators but more as a visual and tactile interface with the computer and an alternative to the WIMP environment (Lister et al., 2003: 114). The Sword of Damocles, as the headset would be known, can be thought of as the first HMD for VR as Sutherland's device allowed for interaction in a computer-generated environment utilising the human body and movement for inputs into the generation of that environment.

Of course, there was no battle between the WIMP environment and early VR—the WIMP environment had already won. The HMD was expen-sive, highly technical and physically uncomfortable. The Sword of Damo-cles had to be suspended from a ceiling due to its weight and during the 1970s, a cable failure during a military experiment resulted in the death of a user (Lanier, 2017: 192). Such a device would have been impractical as an option for a common, commercial computer interface. That it was developed at all, though, is important; from the early 1960s, an important precursor to VR was seen as both an antidote to the dehumanising image of human–computer interactions from early cybernetics and as a method of symbolic interaction with computer systems. A new form of computing had emerged—before its time.

Visual Culture, the Real and the Virtual

Cybernetics posed a pessimistic enough vision of the relationship between humans and computers to provoke a reaction of an embryonic VR system realised in the Sword of Damocles. In the 1980s, Sutherland's response to the cybernetic vision would be the inspiration for the first wave of commer-cial VR—which didn't quite make it to the mass market. While it may seem a simple jump from the Sutherland headset to a vision and drive to com-mercialise VR, this kind of phenomenon does not take place in a vacuum. The development of VR towards working on and developing commercially oriented systems and technology in the 1980s is, like any other techno-logical development, influenced by the culture of the time. The distance between Sutherland's developments in the late 1950s and early 1960s and the wave of VR in the 1980s has more than just a temporal gap; there is also a cultural change across these times that affords the possibility of VR being a legitimate medium that people will spend expertise, time and money on in development.

Simandan (2010) defines cultural studies as a field of theoretically, politically and empirically engaged cultural analysis that concentrates on the political dynamics of contemporary culture, its historical foundations, defining traits, conflicts and contingencies. As such, an approach from cultural studies is ideal for an assessment of the cultural forces that pushed VR from the laboratory and the headset-hanging-from-the-ceiling to the development of systems aimed at a mass market (yet for various reasons not reaching that market at that time). A cultural studies approach can, by definition, help assess that cultural change and what cultural conditions were needed for the emergence (and more importantly hype) of VR as a medium. For brevity, this cultural studies analysis will look at how VR fitted into a wider culture where the virtual and simulation had become a dominant cultural form, drawing on the work of Jean Baudrillard. The aim of this is not to summarise entire cultures or cultural studies (which is impossible with engagement with one major cultural theorist) but to understand how the commercialisation of VR became a possibility thanks to the cultural conditions in which the medium of VR developed.

If one considers VR as a technological innovation (or improvement on other media, an idealisation of the form of visual media), then traditional discourses on technology argue that such improvements are at root an improvement in the efficiency of a technological function. However, in tracing the development of VR, the technical innovations are not simply an increased 'efficiency' of interchange that enable new avenues of investment, increased productivity at work or new domains of leisure and consumption. Instead, those technological developments are in line with a broad and extensive change in *culture*. As Williams (1974) argues, new technologies always reflect and refract the society in which they emerge, and culture emerges from these changed conditions in common life. As VR can be thought of as a computer-generated 'place' that is 'viewed' by the participant through a headset but that responds to stimuli from the participant(s), the term 'virtual reality' corresponds to the observation that one of the features of the 'second media age' (Poster, 1995) is the creation of a simulational culture. In a simulational culture, the processes of mediation have become so intense that the things being mediated are no longer unaffected by those processes of mediation—the mediation of phenomena becomes so dominant that it affects the phenomena itself. VR as a media form is the ideal form of simulation; literally, the medium aims to simulate (rather than replicate) reality.

That contention demands reference to the French sociologist Jean Baudrillard.[2] Baudrillard attempts to conceptualise the transformation of society through an analysis of the dominance of the symbolic over the actual in modern society. In the *Consumer Society* ([1970] 2017), Baudrillard argues that modern culture takes the raw, lived event (the phenomenal) and processes that event into signs. These signs are combined to produce the 'television event', which is in itself not real but which is experienced as real in society as the dominance of the symbolic blocks our understanding of (and access to) the phenomenal. This process of symbolic representation simultaneously actualises and dramatises the real event, producing that event as a spectacle. The result of that transformation of the real to the spectacle is to de-actualise the real, distancing us from the real event. In Baudrillard's words, "we live, sheltered by signs in the denial of the real" (2017: 52). We as media users consume 'the simulation' and experience without the experience of the real at all. In essence, Baudrillard is arguing that the proliferation of signs (in the form of information in the information society) means that we, as consumers, experience more of the world but that experience is purely symbolic—the world itself is transformed into the symbolic through the proliferation of signs. VR as a medium may, at its most ideal, look to replace the real with the symbolic simulation of the real and hence can be seen as a logical end point of Baudrillard's ruminations on the mediatised society in which we live.

This would not be a problem if Baudrillard's words were seen as positive, but of course this is not the case. In *Simulacra and Simulation* ([1981] 2014) Baudrillard introduces the concept of the Simulacrum as something that looks like somebody/something else or that is made to look like somebody/something else. This sounds innocuous, but the combination of signs to form simulacra results in a 'hyperreality' that makes distinguishing truth and falsity impossible. The result of this is an 'implosion' as the growing density of simulations obscures the real completely. This seamless manipulation can be seen in flight simulators (an important application of VR, as will be detailed later in this chapter) in which "the seams between reality and virtuality will be deliberately blurred" (Baudrillard, [1991] 2009: 4). This leads to Baudrillard's famous remark in *The Gulf War Did Not Take Place* that "real tanks can engage simulator crews on real terrain which is simultaneously virtual" (*ibid.*). The real and the simulated cannot be separated—the virtual is everywhere.

Of course, the Gulf War *did* take place, but this notion that the real and simulation cannot be disengaged is important in the context of VR. The argument draws attention to the importance of the virtual in the everyday. In a society where the symbolic dominates the real—where the manipulation of signs has overtaken knowledge of real phenomena—then the virtual is the result of the overabundance of the symbolic. This can be termed the deterrence of the real; the more closely the real is pursued with colour, depth and one technical improvement after another, the greater the distance is between the symbolic and the real and the greater the distance for the media user between the two. So "modern unreality no longer implies the imaginary, it engages more reference, more truth, more exactitude—it consists in having everything pass over into the absolute evidence of the real" (Baudrillard, 1990: 30). The hyperreal is not a case of surrealism but instead should be thought of in terms of a perfection that goes beyond the real and is therefore so *unreal* that it overcomes the real.

One may ask, "What does this have to do with the consumer VR?" Baudrillard's analysis of the dominance of the symbolic in the modern world stresses that "we are no longer in a logic of the passage from virtual to actual but in a hyperrealist logic of the deterrence of the real by the virtual" (Baudrillard, [1991] 2009: 27). In this argument, the virtual has overtaken the actual. The virtual (the state of indistinguishable symbolic and real phenomenal) functions to deter the real event and leaves only a simulacrum of the real. Moreover, Baudrillard stresses that we are not alienated 'spectators' in this cultural process but are 'active agents of the virtual' (Pile and Thrift, 1995: 241). In this sense, as media consumers and as a culture at large, we are complicit in this process as the operators of the virtual, collaborating in our disappearance into the virtual through the continual consumption of the symbolic. So, if we accept this argument, when considering the emergence of VR in the 1980s (and the re-emergence today) the medium emerged into a culture awash with signs and the pre-eminence of the symbolic over the real. VR was not launched into the perfect environment for the crafting of signs over reality; it was a product of the society that already has prioritised the symbolic over the real and realises a value from the cultural fascination with the virtual where the real and the symbolic cannot be distinguished as the symbolic is presented as the real. The market conditions for VR were already there as the condition of replacing the real with the symbolic is a feature of modern society. The creation of a place entirely through computer-generated signs is in itself another, strong attempt to 'cover' the real with the symbolic.

Baudrillard's arguments on the dominance of the symbolic show that as a culture we are ready for VR. VR is the medium that presents a computer-generated reality, and in a society where the real is obscured by the symbolic (and therefore the symbolic is pre-eminent over the real), this fits with the culture of the times. There is a basis for the existence of VR beyond a response to brutal cybernetics. If it is accepted that the culture of the 1970s and 1980s (and, of course, beyond) involved a significant increase in the dominance of the symbolic over the actual, then it contextualises the 1980s VR boom within a wider cultural milieu.

I Say Utopia, You Say Dystopia: The VR Revolution (1.0) of the 1980s

The 1980s and early 1990s were halcyon days of VR in popular culture. The initial wave of commercial VR emerged in the late 1980s through technologists like Jaron Lanier who led the Virtual Programming Languages (VPL) company in San Francisco. VPL was instrumental in developing the first instances of surgical simulations, vehicle interior prototyping and multi-person virtual worlds using an HMD called the EyePhone alongside haptic components called data gloves (Lanier, 2010: 128). (See Figure 2.2.) Lanier has argued that the intention of VPL was to create spontaneous new worlds through VR that would be more expressive and empathetic and 'express the stuff of the mind' (Lanier, 2017: 114), believing that, with the seemingly infinite abundance of everything in virtual worlds, creativity would become especially valuable (Lanier, 2010: 25). As Burbules et al. (2006: 38) summarise succinctly, the goal of VPL was to bring VR to a mass audience.

Figure 2.2 EyePhone and DataGlove

(Source: "Artist Nicole Stenger with VPL EyePhone and DataGlove," Nicole Stenger, 2012, https://commons.wikimedia.org/wiki/File:Nicole_Stenger_Virtual_Reality.jpg)

VPL emerged out of Atari Research, led by Alan Kay and founded in 1982 (Jerald, 2015: 23). The Atari Research team was involved in blue-sky thinking around novel ways of interacting with computers that would prove important in the development of the 1980s generation of VR, as well as developing games. As Lanier (2017: 99–100) notes, VPL research began from the connections and money made designing 8-bit video games for Atari, in particular the psychedelic 1983 game *Moondust*, where the soundtrack was powered by how the player controlled his avatar, a cyber-netic feedback loop in the game that was decidedly symbolic rather than signal. Lanier and Thomas Zimmerman left Atari to form VPL in 1985. One of the most important aspects of the work of VPL was to fix the mate-rial form of VR in popular consciousness through the image of goggles and gloves (La Valle, 2017: 30). As Lanier (2017: 157) notes, the problems of haptics and haptic sensation are core to the possibility of the generality of VR; that is, touch is central to the possibility of VR being a 'general experience machine'. With headsets like the EyePhone or HRX and data gloves, VPL established a visual motif for using VR that makes it look like "you are having interesting experiences but look preposterously nerdy and dorky to onlookers" (Lanier, 2017: 193). The price of these systems was eye-watering at the time and more so today with the prices available for HMDs in the current market. The EyePhone was a $10,000 investment; the HMX—a higher-quality headset that Lanier (2017: 190) suggests had qual-ity akin to the systems of today—cost $50,000; the RB2 or 'Reality built for two' system for co-presence in VR cost approximately $1 million.

The 1980s and 1990s boom in VR followed the work of VPL (although the company filed for bankruptcy in 1990), with customized VR companies such as Virtuality, Division and Fakespace emerging in hardware and soft-ware development (Jerard, 2015: 26) and with major established compa-nies experimenting with the medium. Sega and Nintendo (the two biggest video game console manufacturers in the early 1990s before the emergence of Sony in the market) both expressed interest in VR, and while Sega VR never made the leap to market, the VirtualBoy by Nintendo did in 1995 (not with great success). Nicholas Negroponte, in a message emailed to *Wired Magazine* in 1993, claimed that a $25 HMD was shortly to be introduced and that within five years from 1993, more than one in ten people would be wearing fully mobile HMDs while travelling in buses, trains and planes.

It would be wrong to look at these predictions in a derisive fashion, as the prevailing discourses of the time provided an environment that would have supported these contentions, in themselves based on projections backed by enough venture capital to make them more than realistic. Woolley (1992: 14) recalls the grandiose claims and hyperbole of the SIGGRAPH (Spe-cial Interest Group, Graphics of the American Association of Computer

Machinery) in 1989 and 1990. VR, as it was presented in those events, was not just a way of simulating the real world but a way of building new worlds for consciousness where the constraints of the physical world would be cast away. The idealistic discourses on VR and experimentation with multi-person virtual worlds in the 1980s resonate with John Perry Barlow's manifesto, *A Declaration of the Independence of Cyberspace* (1996). Barlow declared, in response to the Telecommunications 'Reform' Act of 1996, that cyberspace was a world created by collective actions through "transactions, relationships, and thought itself . . . a world that is both everywhere and nowhere, but is not where bodies live" (Barlow, 1996). Cyberspace could transcend the privileges and prejudices of economic power, station of birth and race itself by providing a world where all people, anywhere could express their beliefs freely (Barlow, 1996). This declaration echoed the earlier hopes of VR developers, a form of cyber-utopian dream of a more open world with the help of interconnected, immersive and interactive technologies. The idea that VR could afford a new kind of freedom to the user and to human beings in general was the crux of the utopian ideal of VR that fuelled predictions of VR near-future dominance in the 1990s.

It is easy to criticise Barlow's declaration or the utopianism of VR as being naïve, but these were not immature technology-fuelled ramblings or blunt technological determinism regarding a desire for an improved, countercultural society. The discourses of VR should be considered instead as part of the wider discourses on technology in culture that promise societal as well as technological progress. In the early 1990s, technologists, novelists, pundits and visionaries converged on the idea of VR as a transcendent technology of the near future (Castronova, 2005: 286). This discourse was encoded across contemporary culture; Chesher (1994) discursively analysed research documents and conference papers, publications in magazines, news articles, books, and online postings between 1984 and 1992. Chesher's conclusions were that VR discourses, while positioning VR as new, drew on connections to familiar values, ideologies and myths to position the medium as a natural conclusion to the history of media technologies and a projection into a utopian future (Chesher, 1994: 15–16).

So, VR followed a familiar, teleological discursive path of media technologies and technologies in general. Progress to an end goal of technological utopia goes hand in hand with utopian discourses. During the first wave of commercial VR development, VR also discursively transformed from a marginal and speculative concept into a mainstream and institutionalised discourse within media (Chesher, 1994: 16). Chesher traced this discursive formation through five cultural areas: science fiction, computer history, military development, NASA and counterculture. Though VR's early cultural development began in cyberpunk subculture and computer culture,

journalists and researchers in other fields helped bring it to public attention (Chesher, 1994: 18). VR thereafter "colonized" an array of traditionally
non-computer-based discourses including social science, psychology, philosophy, literature, design, entertainment and art. This colonisation by VR
embedded VR as a discursive object of these forms, representing technological progress, the future and the horizon of human–computer interaction
and cultural consumption. Given this, it is interesting to note how dystopian
these cultural visions of VR were. While the discourses of VR makers were
utopian and drew on and contributed to wider cultural discourses of techno-
utopianism, VR as represented in other media forms was often dangerous,
seedy and criminal.

Strain (1999: 10) calls the representation of speculative forms of VR 'virtual VR', where these representations of VR are blurred with the actual
existing forms of VR and technology. In literature, William Gibson's *Neuromancer* presented a VR dataspace as a space of super-AIs looking to fuse
into a superconsciousness outside the laws of society. Neal Stephenson's
Snow Crash presented the *Metaverse*, a VR-based Internet that resem-
bled a massive-multiplayer-online (MMO) game populated by users and
AI daemons and constituted by a rigid class hierarchy based on the visual
representations of avatars in the VR space. In film, *The Lawnmower Man*[3]
(1992) presented the tale of a man with learning difficulties becoming an
all-powerful, megalomaniacal AI after being absorbed into a VR dataspace
following his use of VR as a test subject. Kathryn Bigelow's 1995 *Strange
Days* presented VR as a seedy technology often involved in the distribution
of 'snuff' experiences. Perhaps the most famous instance of VR in popular
culture, Wachowski's 1999 *The Matrix* positioned VR as a shared, non-
consensual hallucination in the service of an AI using the human race as a
form of energy for its own survival. In the same year, David Cronenberg's
eXistenZ presented a vision of biotechnical virtual reality consoles that
attach to surgically implanted bio-ports but that are the object of ideological
conflict between users and advocates and "realists" that accuse the technology of deforming reality.

On the one hand, discourses within VR development and technological
development in general foresaw not only a bright financial future for the
medium but also a utopian effect of the medium on society. On the other
hand, the representation of and, more importantly, the interpretation of VR
in the arts were often of a dystopian effect of VR use in society. Films and
literature may have cast a misleading sense of the state or soon-to-be state
of VR but this presentation of the medium as dystopian meant that a lack
of fit emerged between technological and cultural discourses on VR. Hayward (1993: 182) argued that such discourses are significant because they
shape both consumer desire for the medium and create an agenda for the

development of the medium. So, on the one hand, designers could be working with an image or agenda of utopian media while the public is developing a quite different image of the possibilities and perceptions of VR. Hayward adds that the effect of the representation of VR in wider culture was to create a simulacrum of the medium itself against which the actual products of VR would have to be compared. At the core of the failure of VR to become a mass market medium in the 1990s was this lack of fit between the expectations (and discourses) of VR and what was on offer. VR never became the $25 HMD medium; the consumer projects that did emerge were chronically disappointing compared to the vision and horizons of the technologists. Cameron (1995: x) observed that the demands made on computing power just to construct the basics of a VR environment in the 1990s were such that VR was barely able to begin representing actual environments. Walsh (1995: 116) viewed the VR of the early 1990s as essentially sterile thanks to the lack of environment generated by the computing of the time. The discourses did not sink VR alone in the 1990s, but the lack of technological power for VR and the popular image of VR in wider culture simply did not fit. The expectation of VR in the 1990s and the 'reality' of VR were incommensurate.

Training, Kickstarting and Control: The Steps to the Re-Emergence of VR

The technological deficiencies of commercial computing meant that the vision of VR for the masses was not realised in the 1990s. Without computers that could support the visual aspects of VR as envisaged by designers and popular culture, commercial VR became trapped in a stasis "waiting for Moore's Law"[4] (Lanier, 2017: 122) to catch up with the demands of the medium through better processing, graphics and memory power. While VR failed to become a low-cost, mass-market entertainment medium, it did become embedded in many fields. Thomas A. Furness III (Henderson, 2015) established the Human Interface Technology Laboratory (HIT Lab) in 1989 at the University of Washington, which produced some of the earliest interdisciplinary VR research for education and training, therapy treatments, pain relief, architecture, archaeology, the ethics of VR and self-identity in virtual worlds. Later, cognitive psychologist and communications professor Jeremy Bailenson founded Stanford University's Virtual Human Interaction Lab (VHIL) in 2003 (Fox, Arena, and Bailenson, 2009). VR would become a critical medium in training, especially in its already established flight simulator mode but also in surgical training and other medical applications (Riener and Harders, 2012). VR would also permeate important developments in wider computational culture. The emergence of

Second Life in 2003, designed by Linden Labs, offered a free-to-access virtual world where users could create avatars and interact with places, other users, objects and explore the open, computer-generated world. It is no surprise that Jaron Lanier and John Perry Barlow were both involved in the development of *Second Life* (Lanier, 2017: 256), given that the application offered the kind of person-centred, experiential formation of digital technology that they had been advocating in the 1990s.

However, *Second Life* was not VR. Experiencing *Second Life* involved viewing the virtual world through the screen of a PC, not an HMD. Moore's Law would not kick in with regard to the kind of computational power available to consumers until the 2010s. In 2011, Palmer Luckey developed the first prototype of the Oculus Rift Virtual Reality (VR) headset, an HMD offering a platform for the delivery of the kind of VR experience that would match the visions and imaginaries of the 1990s. On 1 August 2012, Luckey's Oculus VR launched a Kickstarter crowd-funding campaign that raised $2,437,429 in 30 days for the development of this prototype into the first commercially available Oculus headset (Kickstarter, 2012). Harris's (2018) account of the movement of enthusiasts and developers that resurrected VR during this time emphasises both the outsider nature of this development and the incorporation of the vision into Silicon Valley. Oculus did not prove to be the beginning of a VR home-brewed revolution. While technology had caught up with the vision of VR, the wider cultural context that digital technology framed VR in during the 2010s meant that the utopian vision of VR would now be accommodated in a digital eco-structure dominated by organisations driven by very specific aims and objectives. Chapter 3 argues that the world in which VR is re-emerging is very different from the world in which it developed in the 1990s, and this may have profound effects on the form and function of the medium.

Notes

1. Coined at the Dartmouth Conference in 1959 (Lanier, 2017: 57).
2. See Merrin (2005) for a comprehensive discussion of Baudrillard's theoretical engagement with modern media.
3. Apparently adapted from a short story by Stephen King, but which bears no resemblance at all to the source material. Interestingly, VPL's EyePhone HMD appears in the film.
4. Moore's Law is the observation, by Gordon Moore (1965), that the processing power of computers would double approximately every two years as a function of the doubling of the number of transistors in an integrated circuit over that period. Computational power is contingent on these transistors.

3   The VR Business Model

The previous chapter leaves us with the emergence of the Oculus Rift in 2012. The Rift and other developments in VR, such as the Google Cardboard, PSVR, HTC Vive and Vive Focus, Oculus Go and Lenovo Mirage, have not been thrown into a world from the heavens with no context to their development or place within a wider digital media eco-structure. In the 2010s, we live in an advanced digital media environment where computational devices are our everyday companions and are entangled in our lives in a number of ways, in a complex social milieu that reflects our wider society that depends on information and data (Berry, 2011: 3). This wider cultural context in which VR has re-emerged as a consumer medium is a critically important factor in the shaping of VR and what VR will be for consumers if it becomes a part of our everyday media experience. The purpose of this chapter is to critically assess what effect the wider socio-technical context may have on VR, with a focus on the companies that have invested considerable capital into VR-based enterprises: Facebook, Samsung, Google, Microsoft, Sony and HTC.

This wider socio-technical context is important because of how these major digital media companies operate, what their strategic goals are and how VR may be used by companies to achieve these goals. These digital behemoths are not backing VR or investing heavily in hardware, platforms and software for altruistic or nostalgic reasons. The promise of VR as a medium that offers unparalleled immersion in virtual environments brings other tangible benefits to the companies in question: a platform to both dictate content and closely monitor and measure user preference (through means and methods not achievable with current media devices); the possibility of creating virtual worlds that can be controlled by companies and be harvested for data on users by companies; the possibility at this new dawn of establishing monopoly positions in terms of hardware and operating platform in a new media field with considerable allure for consumers. Control. The presence of major companies that base their business models on mass data collection and processing or on monopoly-chasing positions in software and gaming is hardly surprising when a position of control is wide open in the new consumer VR market.

Technological Lag and the Digital Media Giants

In the introduction to this book, an argument was developed that the reason that the first wave of VR in the 1980s and 1990s failed was due to a technological lag. This simple concept means that the visions and imaginaries of VR in that time could not be realised through the consumer technology available then. The notion of a cultural lag is well established (Woodard, 1934), this being the phenomenon whereby culture takes time to catch up with technological innovations and that social problems and conflicts are caused by this lag. A technological lag still involves a critical delay, but this is in the technology rather than in the social and cultural aspects of society that are forced to react to the presence of a new technology. In a technological lag, a proposed technology may be critically delayed, and within that delay period, society itself has undergone considerable changes, which then affect the implementation or use of the technology itself in comparison with the initial vision.

This chapter will use this initial notion of a technological lag to understand and problematise the re-emergence of VR in the 2010s in the context of the socio-technical culture into which it is re-emerging as a legitimate consumer medium. Prior to that, though, it is necessary to understand how the technological lag has been overcome. Put simply, there are two key properties of technology in the re-emergence of VR: power and adaption. The 'high-end' integrated VR experiences such as the PSVR, HTC Vive, Windows Mixed Reality and Oculus Rift are possible thanks to power. The stand-alone HMDs released for a push to consumer uptake in 2018, the Oculus Go and Lenovo Mirage, are variants on the Gear (developed by Oculus) and Google Daydream mobile platforms, which allow for VR experiences without a powerful PC—and untethered VR experience—utilising a Qualcomm Snapdragon 821 chip used in smartphones but without the demands that smartphones put on this hardware. Innovative mobile VR platforms such as the Google Cardboard and Daydream and the Samsung Gear are possible thanks to adaption of other technologies. Power specifically refers to the processing affordances of consumer computers that allow for a high-quality VR experience to be made available to consumers. The PSVR relies on the PlayStation 4, an eighth-generation console with sufficient processing power to deliver VR. The Oculus Rift, Windows Mixed Reality and HTC Vive platforms rely on high-powered PCs with advanced graphics capabilities and processing power in order to run. The need for this is obvious: any drops in frame rates or resolution when using these headsets would be disastrous in terms of the nausea-inducing experience that the VR environment would provoke. The need for processing power is not limited to graphics—integrated VR systems also require tracking systems and haptic interfaces or game controllers, the data from which needs to be processed in real time with the graphical interface to maintain the integrity of the VR experience.

These VR platforms have effectively been 'waiting for Moore's Law' (Lanier, 2017: 122); the development of fully integrated VR platforms for consumer VR has involved waiting for commercially available PCs to catch up with the vision of early VR in terms of processing power, memory and connectivity to platforms. This has been a piecemeal process; connectivity has not been an issue since the late 1990s, but sufficient memory and processing power has been (in the consumer market) available only since the late 2000s. The kind of processing power needed for running these VR systems is relatively still expensive, as one of the major barriers to VR adoption in the early stage of this wave of VR has been the expense of a PC that is capable of running VR. A machine that can provide the minimum specifications for VR ranges from £800 to £2000; with the cost of an HMD, the outlay of over £1000 at a minimum for high-end VR is expensive in comparison to eighth-generation game consoles or other consumer entertainment media. Despite this cost, the emergence of high-powered processors (CPU), graphics cards (GPU), sufficient random-access memory (RAM) and video output ports in home computers has facilitated integrated, high-quality VR overcoming the technological boundary to adoption in the commercial market and seen the emergence of genuine VR experiences in the consumer media market. With the emergence of low-cost but less powerful consumer VR HMDs in 2018, such as the Oculus Go and Lenovo Mirage, the Rubicon of consumer VR may finally have been crossed.

Once these necessary PC-based elements of consumer VR became part of the consumer computing market, there was still a requirement for the development of consumer VR hardware, software and a platform to link these two elements together. The first company to emerge in this space was Oculus. Oculus was founded in 2012 and found instant fame through the Kickstarter campaign mentioned in Chapter 2. That campaign made an early prototype HMD available to developers, which shipped in March 2013 (Oculus, 2012). The release to developers is an indication of the kind of technological development that the Rift is, in that software must be custom programmed to use the Rift. From the outset of the project, the vision for the Rift was not just for an affordable consumer VR headset that produced a VR experience akin to the state-of-the-art equipment in laboratories like the Stanford University Virtual Human Interactive Lab (Bailenson, 2018:

7). The Oculus model of VR provision was to produce the hardware and to control the software through programming specificity and control of the platform through their Oculus Home VR interface. While games and VR experiences are also available through the Steam digital distribution platform (Steam VR was launched in 2016, after the commercial launch of the Oculus Rift), there remains a level of control built into the Rift as a technological assemblage of hardware, platform and software. The Rift would not become commercially available until January 2016, but from 2012 the 'buzz' around the new wave of VR was established by the emergence of Oculus.

In Oculus's wake, others followed. HTC, in partnership with Valve (the owners of the Steam platform) revealed the Vive headset in early 2015 prior to the consumer release of the headset in April 2016. The set-up of this system is similar to the Rift; an HMD with controllers both tracked by base stations, with software available through the Viveport platform and the Steam platform. Both Oculus and the HTC Vive have a software distribution model based on the app store model that first emerged in Apple's iOS platform in 2007. Microsoft's Windows Mixed Reality systems also utilise software distribution through the Microsoft Store as well as the Steam platform. Sony, of course, has a similar platform available for the PSVR via the PlayStation store. The 'high-end' VR market that has emerged since 2012 has been a utilisation not just of the processing and memory power of contemporary consumer computing but also of the digital distribution model for software and closed, proprietary platform home areas where control of the software for the system can be exercised. These platforms have expanded in 2018, with the emergence of stand-alone HMDs for the consumer market. The Oculus Go has a reshaped but retained Oculus Home for software; the Lenovo Mirage uses the Google Daydream infrastructure; the HTC Vive Focus uses the Viveport platform. These are closed, proprietary platforms from three major companies competing for exclusive domination of the emerging consumer VR market.

At the opposite end of the emerging consumer VR market, the key innovation has been in the adaptability of smartphones in providing lower-cost VR options. The enclosing of a smartphone in a simple case that holds the phone at a set distance from the eyes has been key to opening up VR to many consumers since 2014 (LaValle, 2017: 8). Google's Cardboard platform was a low-cost system that replicates the same principles as the Brewster stereoscope more than 150 years earlier. Google also provided a software development kit (SDK) for developers on both their own Android operating system and the iOS system for smartphones. Bailenson (2018: 8) argues that entry-level systems like Cardboard and Samsung's Gear (developed in conjunction with Oculus), which commonly deliver 360° video or very limited immersive experiences, may not technically qualify as VR. These platforms deliver environments that are more passive and involve less movement than those that can be developed in more technologically advanced systems. As detailed in Chapter 1, VR is argued as requiring digitally created environments that have an immersive effect through the assemblage of different immersive elements, and so smartphone-based platforms at least have the possibility of being considered as VR.

While the hardware involved in these platforms is far less technologically advanced—notwithstanding the need for a sophisticated smartphone, which can mean that VR delivered on these platforms can be expensive—the software distribution model is remarkably similar to the PC-tethered platforms. Apps that support Cardboard are available through the Google Play store or App Store for iOS, which is optimal given the need for a smartphone as a basis for the platform. The ability of smartphones to handle graphics, video and audio in a sophisticated manner through these apps is the basis for the Cardboard-based VR platforms. Innovation in this case was simply recognising the affordances of smartphone technology and adapting historic ideas on visual media—which has realised sales of 10 million units and 160 million app downloads (Jonnalagadda, 2017).

So, the technological aspect of the technological lag in consumer VR has been overcome, but the concept of the technological lag is not exclusively concerned with improvements in transistor chips or orienting smartphones appropriately. The development of the Rift was an example of a particularly sophisticated home-brewed computing development. While Palmer Luckey was a self-taught engineer, he was mentored by Mark Bolas from the University of Southern California (Bailenson, 2018: 7), who created the first 150° field of view HMD in 2006 and whose MxR laboratory won the best demo award at the 2012 IEEE VR conference (Jerald, 2015: 27). The Rift was developed after Luckey left the lab shortly after this event, and although the hacker community and media once again showed an interest in VR following the Kickstarter campaign for the Rift, the possibility of a repeat of the idealistic wave of VR development and visions from the 1980s did not last long. In 2014, while the Rift was still only available as a development model, Facebook announced they were acquiring Oculus for $2 billion. Gleasure and Feller (2016: 708) note that this move caused considerable consternation among many of the original backers of the project, in no small part due to who was buying the company.

A cursory glance at the companies that have been involved in overcoming the technological barriers to consumer VR illustrates the essence of the technological lag, which was at the root of the bad feeling about the Oculus takeover: Facebook, Google, Samsung, Microsoft, HTC. These companies share a particular set of values and positions in the digital economy and digital culture that makes their already dominant presence in VR an issue. At root, the technological lag has seen the countercultural idealism of the 1980s and 1990s wave of VR development replaced by giant digital media companies looking to dominate a new platform in line with ideologies of control and disruption that are the trademark of some and the aspiration of others. The technological lag in VR has meant that VR has re-emerged into a digital media environment where these organisations are not only dominant but are also looking to consolidate and develop their dominance in their own fields of the digital economy. It is no accident that these major companies are at the forefront of the consumer VR market; the concept of the technological lag requires an understanding of their aims, business models, ideological concerns and visions for VR to assess what kind of medium VR is becoming as a result of the long winter of consumer VR between the early 1990s and early 2010s.

Digital Oil: Data and the Weaponisation of the Web

The presence of the modern digital giants is an issue in the re-emergence of VR because of the very environment that these companies have created from their primary medium, the World Wide Web. When the inventor of this medium, Tim Berners-Lee (2018), claims that the Web itself is under threat from misinformation, questionable practices of political advertising, a loss of control over personal information and the weaponisation of the Web by these major companies, then there are indications that the emerging dominance of these organisations in VR deserves attention. By weaponisation, Berners-Lee is referring to the use of data harvested and analysed by Facebook and others and then deployed as tools for political gain, such as the Facebook data breach used by Cambridge Analytica to target and manipulate Facebook users. The algorithms at work on the Facebook platform trawl through the interactions and activities of users on the platform to gather sensitive personal information about sexual orientation, race, gender, intelligence and even childhood trauma—mining and refining the 'digital oil' (Humby, 2006 in Palmer, 2006) of the digital economy. These results can then be used to target users with tailored information to play on this psychological and personal profile in order to attempt to persuade users to take particular courses of action (Cadwalladr and Graham-Harrison, 2018). At root, Berners-Lee's concerns are around polarisation of the Web (Solon, 2018) and the dominance of a few companies in a medium that was designed for and bloomed through an environment of universal usage and access. As Jaron Lanier (2014: 348) argued, the digital world has become remarkably consolidated. While the World Wide Web was often portrayed "as a great wilderness of teeming, mysterious activities, it is actually mostly supervised by a small number of companies." The dominance of these companies has afforded them the opportunity to become vast data aggregators with the potential to disrupt and be disrupted in the context of wider society. Without monopolistic positions in search and data organisations (Google), social networking (Facebook) or operating systems for PCs (Microsoft), there would not exist the affordances for the kinds of control and polarisation that cause these concerns. The Web and networked activity are dominated by a few companies—and, of course, these are the companies that are beginning to stake out positions of dominance in VR.

The issues for VR emerge when VR is conceptualised as a medium that is (like other mediums, such as the Web) not just a technology but a socio-technical system. Like other mediums, VR has a technological level of artefacts (HMDs, controllers, connections, etc.) that enable and constrain a social level of human activities. These activities that are defined in scope by the medium itself create knowledge that is produced, diffused and consumed with the help of the artefacts of the technological level (Fuchs, 2015: 39). Therefore, there is always a recursive dynamic relationship or a feedback loop between the technological and the social levels of any media being used. According to Anthony Giddens (1984), media have the duality of structure and agency; media provide the structure of social systems and define the agency that individuals have in social systems through enabling and constraining actions. So, media are socio-technical systems that enable and constrain human activities and that create knowledge that is produced, distributed and consumed with the help of the same technologies in a dynamic and reflexive process that connects technological structures and human agency (Fuchs, 2015: 39).

The effect of media in this context is therefore to structure human agency within the logics of a particular technological system. With regard to the media that are produced, controlled and monopolised by the digital media giants, Lanier (2014: 79) argues that the information economy that we are currently building does not embrace capitalism as an economic system of participation, but rather it is a new form of feudalism where users are farmed for data and their interactions with one another become the foundation of a new data economy. Companies like Facebook organise data from users for the benefit of remote clients who want to manipulate what is presented to those people over those very networks (Lanier, 2014: 313). The result of this is that the process of capital accumulation itself in corporate digital media platforms is targeted advertising dictated by user activity (Nieborg and Poell, 2018). The role of the media in the past has been to control and harness that audience power to produce a commodity that can be produced, sold and consumed (Smythe, 2001). Advertisers in effect buy attention as a product from platforms committed to the monopolisation of attention

(Wu, 2017). This is sold by others, not by you, despite you doing the 'work'. The difference between 'old' media and digital media is that 'attention' can be quantified much more closely and specifically. The platforms of digital media allow for the storage and analysis of all interactions on those platforms; every search, every like, every message and every click-through can be saved and added to the churn of data harvesting on the data subject created by the systems that view users through the lens of user interaction. It is here that the investment in VR by these companies becomes problematic. VR is a medium where attention hacking (Abi-Heila, 2018) is unnecessary because attention is a given as a VR headset acts as an isolation chamber for sight, hearing and haptic senses. A medium that promises advanced and revolutionary innovation also promises other means and methods of data aggregation. Consider, for example, the use of eye tracking in VR headsets (Hardawa, 2018). For VR users, eye tracking in HMDs affords focus and a sense of intentionality for the VR avatar that cannot be communicated via hand controllers, as well as being essential to the understanding of positioning of the user in the VR environment for programmers and developers. Eye tracking also provides a data point for the gaze of the eyes in a virtual environment. In an environment saturated with targeted advertising, that data on gaze can inform about the effectiveness of particular advertising and can quantify 'attention' in a new manner that is not even possible in the data harvesting environments of digital media.

Given Facebook's ownership of Oculus, a focus on the critique of that company here is useful. In general, critiques of the major digital media companies have convalesced around the exploitation of users for data—but this is explicitly a focus of any critique of Facebook. Online advertising has been seen as a mechanism by which Facebook exploits users as users become a commodity (Fuchs, 2008, 2010). Web 2.0 in general has been seen as based on the exploitation of free labour (Terranova, 2004), but Facebook has perfected this exploitation. Under the conditions of use of the platform, most users become part of a creative precarious underclass of labourers whose 'work' is dictated by and for the benefit of the platform that they use (Lovink, 2008; Jarrett, 2016). This economy is dominated by a few corporate media companies (Stanyer, 2009) that use the notion of 'sharing' for mystifying the logic of profit, advertising and commerce that is at the heart of their operation (John, 2012)—with Facebook being an ideal example.

Evgeny Morozov crystallises these criticisms. Optimism around social media is based on the techno-deterministic ideologies of cyber-utopianism (Morozov, 2011) that only postulate advantages for businesses and society through the lens of that industry and the benefits to that industry without taking into account the realities of exploitation and the contradictions of capitalism. José van Dijck (2013: 11) argues that social media achieves this through an automation of the social by engineering and manipulating social connections. Douglas Rushkoff (2010: 158) argues that as a result of this, social media is involved in a process of "optimizing humans for machinery". Christian Fuchs (2015: 15) summarises why this is so problematic. Facebook is a company controlled by private shareholders who own the Facebook platform. Facebook's users create data whenever they are online that refers to their profiles and online behaviour. This data is sold to Facebook's advertising clients who are enabled to present targeted advertisements on users' profiles. Without Facebook users, there would be no profit. So, users create the monetary value and profit of Facebook, but they do not own this profit, which is controlled by Facebook's shareholders. Facebook users are exploited. Indeed, social media prosumers are double objects of commodification: they are commodities themselves, and through this commodification their consciousness (as embodied through their activity) becomes, while online, permanently exposed to commodity logic in the form of advertisements (Fuchs, 2015: 160).

The effect of this commercial model is to capture extremely valuable information that is made valuable through use. Using this information, an advertiser might hypothetically be able to target all the members of a peer group just as they are forming their opinions about brands, habits and so on. (Lanier, 2010). Karppi and Crawford (2015: 73–74) identify that the processes used by social media are similar to others used in modern capitalism. Social media and financial algorithms are linked as they are part of the same overall eco-structure. In this sense, social media connects human communicative spaces to automated computational spaces. When reflecting on the trajectories of Oculus, the 'weaponisation' of VR in this model is fairly obvious. VR presents another medium or platform to be enrolled in this process of data accumulation and algorithmic profiling for the efficiency of the commercial model of targeted advertising. Indeed, the creation of a purely computational space for social media affords the possibility of the deployment of data collection and algorithmic measurement in an environment where perception and bodily movement can be measured, where currently these cannot be measured in the same way, only implied. Facebook Spaces (the VR version of Facebook) can act as a fully integrated dataspace—a space of data harvesting and processing in the way that the Facebook platform operates but with greater efficiency if the promises of immersion in space that VR has always supported can be realised. Every interaction, gesture, glance and pause in the VR environment can be measured and quantified to add to the profile for advertisers.

Digital Gods and Monsters

It would be wrong to suggest that Facebook is an outlier in this critique (Taplin, 2017). Google's model of operation can be argued to be constant real-time bio-political exploitation. Hardt and Negri (2000: 24) have argued that the contemporary capitalism of which Google is a foundational part is based on a form of Foucauldian bio-power. Google's vision is one where the world is made completely knowable, controllable and predictable. Google are therefore proponents of an ideology that Evgeny Morozov (2013: 5) calls "technological solutionism". Solutionism is a recasting of all complex social situations either as neatly defined problems with definite, computable solutions or as transparent and self-evident processes that can be easily optimised—if only the right algorithms are in place. Morozov (2013: 43) argues that solutionism is a typical ideology of Silicon Valley entrepreneurs and intellectuals who glorify digital media as being the solution to societal problems. Technological solutionism reimagines the individual and the social as part of the algorithms or systems of digital media, and therefore any problems arising at an individual or social level can be solved by these digital media. This notion clearly has roots in cybernetic theory, as well as exerting a form of bio-power where individuals are subjugated under these systems in order to create new data subjects. Google can be seen as a control machine that aims at controlling people's perception of reality and at transforming these perceptions into profits (Fuchs, 2015: 162). The implication here for VR is more stark even than the vision posited through the critique of Facebook: a company that desires to make the world knowable has a platform in VR where worlds themselves can be constructed. The VR world made by such a company will include the information that they choose to include, that fits into their ideological frame and that augments their aims of organising and ordering the world in a manner that benefits them as an organisation.

The privacy of individuals using these platforms is a root cause of much of the consternation about the wider influence of these digital giants. Helen Nissenbaum argues that the "right to privacy is neither a right to secrecy nor a right to control but a right to appropriate flow of personal information" (Nissenbaum, 2010: 127). However, it is these flows of information that remain opaque and hidden from circumspection. Surveillance on Facebook for example is surveillance of prosumers, who dynamically and permanently create and share user-generated content, browse profiles and data, interact with others, join, create, and build communities and co-create information (Fuchs, 2015). While Oculus might claim that they are independent from Facebook and that they do not share data with Facebook, their privacy policy allows for this as it is written in an open-ended manner that does not disclose how data is captured, stored or shared (Bye, 2018). The usage of such platforms creates a trail of breadcrumbs that form a picture of a data subject that is sold to advertisers as an unavoidable consequence of engagement with the platform itself—and VR may contribute to this in new and unexpected ways. Businesses that make money by collecting and selling detailed records of private lives were once plainly described as "surveillance companies". Their rebranding as "social media" recognises that people are willing to agree to a power relationship with these companies in return for the facilities that are offered by surveillance platforms. One can inform oneself about the issues with surveillance, but the reason no one reads the fine print is that even if you do take the time, there will soon be a new revision, and reading the fine print becomes a full-time job (Lanier, 2014: 314).

The prime 'oil' for these companies is the billions of identities they mine and get to know in ever greater detail. The core of the business model is the easy access to that core material. In comparison, virtual reality represents a business risk, unless that medium is enrolled into the primary business model. If people make it clear, with their clicks, likes, and postings, that they hate certain things and love others, those people are easy to sell to (Galloway, 2017). If this can be done in virtual environments accessed through VR platforms designed, operated and controlled by Facebook, Google or any other digital giant, then the possibilities of the integration of VR into this vast data machine are clear. As Galloway (2017) argues, the companies will continue with more of the same. With global reach, near-limitless capital and its ever smarter data-crunching AI machines, Facebook and Google will lay waste to any competition and dictate the development of media in this era.

Michel Foucault argued that power is not only located in powerful bodies such as the state or companies. Power produces reality, "it produces domains of objects and rituals of truth. The individual and the knowledge that may be gained of him belong to this production" (Foucault, 1977: 250). The corporate platforms owned by Facebook, Google and other large companies not only strongly mediate the cultural expressions of Internet users (Fuchs, 2015: 68) but are involved in the creation of our realities themselves—and, in the context of VR, are literally involved in the creation of alternate computational realities. While this discussion has focussed on these giants, it's easy to forget that Microsoft dominates the operating systems market and is competing in the VR space with Sony in a mirror battle of their conflict in the games console market. HTC is a major smartphone manufacturer with a scale that could easily benefit from an explosion in data-driven commerce. These companies are all in the same digital market space, looking for a competitive advantage to consolidate and improve market share in an economy where data is a critical commodity. VR provides another avenue not only to exercise a monopoly position but to collect data on users—and data of a new kind to boot.

The New Capitalism: Platforms, Attention and Ideology

To return this discussion to the re-emergence of VR, the medium is re-emerging into a wider context where a few companies dominate the digital economy, and their dominance is predicated on establishing and maintaining vast data harvesting facilities that allow for the generation of vast revenues. The investment of a small portion of these revenues into VR may be seen as an offsetting of potential risk or an indulgence of hobbyists, but, should the re-emergence of VR be successful in the way that it was envisaged as a game-changing medium in the 1980s (and is still today with regard to discourses of immersion), then these companies are positioning themselves early in the development cycle of a new medium that can extend their operational parameters. This resonates with Srnicek's (2016) notion of platform capitalism where capitalism itself is involved in a continual enrolment of new technologies to increase efficiencies and improve the processes of capital accumulation. VR fits with these platforms in a manner that complements their primary functions, as part of an eco-structure of data collection. These platforms have positioned themselves as user-centred platforms for improving the efficiency of everyday life and have been enrolled into the everyday lives of people accordingly. The word 'social' associated with media implies that platforms are user centred and that they facilitate communal activities, just as the term 'participatory' emphasises human collaboration. Social media can be seen as online facilitators or enhancers of human networks (Van Dijck, 2013: 11). However, as a result of the interconnection of platforms, a new infrastructure has emerged: an ecosystem of connective media with a few large and many small players creating a 'platformed' sociality (Van Dijck, 2013: 4).

The disruption caused by such platforms (in terms of privacy, disruption to democratic processes and decision making) has often been conceptualised ideologically through Barbrook and Cameron's (1996) concept of the Californian Ideology. This has been thought of as the ideology of the techno-elite in Silicon Valley, a radical mixture of libertarian and the radical politics of the 60s counterculture. Formulaically, the ideology can be expressed as a combination of 'let me do what I want' and 'don't tax me' = Facebook, Amazon, Google and others. In practice, this ideology manifests itself in the forms of new media and the ownership models of new media where vast profits are made from the exploitation of user-generated data with a business model that avoids corporate taxes and a social responsibility attitude that avoids accountability for the actions of actors on platforms. This ideological position on the operations of companies goes some way to explaining the vast data harvesting operations on the Facebook platform (Lewis, 2018) in light of the Cambridge Analytica scandal around the 2016 U.S. election and 2016 Brexit referendum, where user profiles were extensively analysed and targeted with specific, psychologically affecting content in order to influence voting patterns. What the Californian Ideology does not emphasise, though, is the brutal instrumentalism of these platform in conceptualising users—they are raw materials to be transformed into data (the commodity form) to be sold and to hell with the consequences.

With that instrumentalisation in mind, the platformed use of human beings becomes clear, and the role of VR in these models should become clearer. The question of the utility of VR to the digital giants is, "What can VR do in terms of creating data on users to be used in this economic model?" Andrew Keen (2017) notes that the problem with the digital community in general is that it is dominated by a few companies, but critically the medium of exchange among these companies is the attention economy. This economy is a product of the use of the products of these dominant companies. With a medium that promises unparalleled immersion in worlds that can be designed, branded, controlled and economically ordered by these digital giants, VR does appear to have a distinct relationship to the business models of dominant companies in the digital economy. The priorities of these companies are currently clicks, numbers, time on site and retaining attention as a way of increasing the amount of data in a profile. As long ago as 1965, Gary Becker was arguing that time, not material goods, is the key scarcity in modern society. The attention economy is based on that fundamental principle. James Ash (2015: 99) rightly notes that attention is referent not just to the immediate and real time but also to the past and the present. The key to the attention economy is to create an environment where the attention paid in the present can refer to a past and a future within a given experience or platform. The modulation of focus therefore requires a historical aspect and a future aspect. Within this, the dominance of the digital giants in the attention economy becomes clear; their ubiquity through utility transforms into a historical relationship and a perceived future relationship that modulates the attention of the given time. VR provides a new and potentially vast opportunity to capture attention in an immersive virtual environment that offers new quantifications and therefore economic possibilities with users.

The Digital Skinner Box

Lanier (2017: 62) offers a 13th definition of VR as VR being possibly the perfect digital Skinner Box. This is not meant as a compliment. A Skinner Box refers to the operant conditioning chamber designed by B. F. Skinner to create a deliberatively restrictive environment where behaviours can be shaped through the manipulation of stimuli and reward and punishment mechanisms to determine behavioural responses. If VR can be utilised as an apparatus for the extension of the quantification of the everyday—a medium where everything can and will be measured—then the design and build of both VR equipment and experiences will be to optimise that need for quantification. Moreover, in the hands of companies that already exploit algorithms for altering the mood of users (Meyer, 2014) and harvest data on an industrial scale, VR represents a new medium that can extend and perfect these drives for control. If VR is used as an operant conditioning chamber that can be used to harvest personal information while also directing users to particular choices (political, social, commercial or any other that can be conceptualised in a virtual environment), then VR itself is a danger. This may sound hyperbolic, but the historical and current discourses of VR are about the revolutionary immersive properties of the medium in comparison to other mediums used by people. A medium where the user feels totally at home yet is in a world entirely made by and controlled by an organisation that is looking to collect data for sale (and may be comfortable with other organisations accessing their platform for more nefarious reasons, such as Cambridge Analytica) may make current unease with social media big data seem like a quaint set of worries—if VR takes off commercially as these companies might hope.

Galloway (2017) argues that the drive into VR by Facebook, Google, Microsoft and others is an extension of the fight for market dominance and an example of these companies making bold bets on the future of the digital economy. Google's vision is in organising the world's information. Facebook's vision is in 'connecting the world'. Thanks to the economies of scale and economic success that both companies have already achieved in these areas, both can afford to gamble on VR as initially an additional part of the business. Should VR ever fulfil some of the more advanced ambitions of being a new form of computing or interface with computing altogether, then the presence of these companies (along with Microsoft as the dominant OS provider globally) in the field becomes more obvious. As Castells (1996: 17) argued, in the informational mode of development, the source of productivity lies in the technology of knowledge generation, information processing and symbolic communication, all of which VR can play a role in. Bratton (2016: 56) furthers this critique, noting that the accidental megastructure (or 'stack') that emerges from the planetary-scaled computation that the digital giants are a fundamental part of enmeshes both users and interfaces. It is not a surprise, then, that the organisations that are fundamental to this level of computation are dominant in a re-emerging form of HCI: a medium that can allow a world based on data and programming principles to be built and that then allows for the closest scrutiny of users with regard to both data harvesting and targeted advertising. The perfect storm.

As for the fears raised in this chapter over the business models of some of the main players now in the VR space, these fears are largely obvious. As Beer (2015: 1) states, big data is central to the working of contemporary capitalism and a facilitator of neo-liberalism. It forms the backdrop to market operations and as such is an integrated part of everyday culture even if the calculative and computational form of its operations remain opaque. Calculation is grounded in the science of knowledge of the mathematical and is set into power by the machinery of technology. Above all, calculation requires all things to be shifted to be calculable. This ordering of things is facilitated by technology (Elden, 2003: 41). VR as a technology may therefore be used in the shifting of more things to the calculable—attention, gaze, interaction, gesture, anything that can be sensed through a VR interface. In this sense, VR will not exist to satisfy human needs, but human behaviour will have to be modified to fit the needs of the system (Kelly, 2011: 198, citing the Unabomber, Ted Kaczynski). If the original system that VR must fit with is designed with an ideology at play, then the need for an enrolment of users in the system is in itself ideological. When these companies invested heavily in VR, we already knew to an extent that they saw the medium as an extension of the means to calculate and create, analyse and sell data commercially.

So, in overcoming the technological lag of VR, VR as a medium has been cast into a new environment where the dominant companies are involved in data collection on a planetary (rather than an industrial) scale. While the argument presented in this chapter might seem tangential to VR, these digital giants have crushed the idealism of the early Web (as exemplified in John Perry Barlow's declaration) and replaced this with a concentration of power based on control of data. While some theorists (Bailenson, 2018: 220) maintain that "VR is a democracy", an equally valid alternative is that VR may be the *most* undemocratic medium (Tinnell, 2018), thanks to the myriad barriers to commercial VR and the presence of the data giants in the field. These companies have particular politics and ideologies that seek market domination, control of both information and data and an attitude of disruption that allows for the circumvention of norms and societal values (without considering other questionable elements of the culture of Silicon Valley, such as Emily Chang's (2018) characterisation of a *Brotopia*, where Silicon Valley is a modern utopia where anyone can change the rules or make their own rules, as long as they are a man). As Keen (2018) argues following his interview with Chris Hughes, a co-founder Facebook, these companies are undermining the 'American Dream' itself through a winner-takes-all mentality that squeezes both competition and innovation. VR has leapfrogged into a future where the dominant companies and dominant economic model is one where the user is the product to be harvested and sold as a commodity through the abstractions made on platforms with multiple data points. VR adds to these data points in a number of interesting and potentially valuable ways. However, there will be no digital Skinner Box if VR is not a success and if the promise of deep, immersive experience that is genuinely revolutionary cannot be met. The next chapter explores this critical aspect in more detail.

4 Immersion, or the Unique Selling Point of VR

VR is the ability to take a user through currently the senses of sights, sound and touch and place them within a computer based environment that fools them into believing they are somewhere else other than the real world.
—James, director of Immersive Technologies

I could sit watching my partner play the VR game *Job Simulator* for hours. The game involves performing a series of mundane and absurd tasks in various work-based environments, such as respraying cars, making rudimentary meals or being a cubicle-based office drone. While the game looks more like the seminal Dire Straits video *Money for Nothing* than a realistic office, diner or garage, the realism of the graphics seem to have no impact on the effect of the game. When I play the game and when my partner plays the game, there is an immersion in that computer-generated environment based on the activity, interaction with objects and computer-generated characters, sounds and feeling that are derived from 'being-there' in the *Job Simulator*. The fact that you often receive more positive feedback and job-related satisfaction from the experience is also very helpful. The immersion in *Job Simulator* is such that I eventually (well, after a few minutes) start yelling at the unresponsive voice and animated robots that make continual demands on me as a wageless but eager employee. When I am in that situation, I am experiencing a high degree of immersion in the experience. I'm moving food, dishes, car parts using my PS Move controllers, I'm listening to instructions and mundane background tunes and trying to achieve my goals set by the game.

As Bailenson (2018: 5) states, experience is doing something, and in *Job Simulator* I am doing something. My experience, as well as that of my partner and others I have seen playing *Job Simulator*, is immersive. A critical aspect of the commercial appeal of VR stems from the idea that VR is a medium that *immerses* the user to an extent that they feel they are somewhere *else*. Given much of the coverage and commentary on VR, a naïve observer would be excused for thinking that immersion is a given with VR, such is the ubiquity of the word in advertising and promotion of the medium. This chapter argues that immersion is far from a given and that the ultimate goal of achieving immersion consists of combining a number of elements of different sensory stimuli and preparedness on the part of the VR user to be immersed. Immersion is reframed here as a tightly crafted emergent property of the visuals, sounds, narratives and haptics (or touch) of the VR experience and the mood or orientation of the user towards the VR experience itself. While some of these elements might be more prevalent than others in an immersive experience, some might be missing altogether, and immersion might still take place as immersion emerges from the interplay and combination of these elements.

Immersion and Presence

Slater and Wilbur (1997) argue that immersion is the degree to which VR projects stimuli onto the sensory receptors of VR users in a way that is extensive, matching (i.e., has congruence or resemblance between different sensory modalities), surrounding, vivid, interactive and plot forming. A VR project will always have two parts, though: the project and a user (hopefully) having a subjective experience of immersion. Jerald (2015: 46–47) defines this subjective feeling of immersion as presence. Presence is the sense of 'being there' in a particular space, and in the context of VR that sense is of being in a space or world that is in a different location from the one that we are physically in at that time. The immersive qualities or properties of the VR experience can facilitate presence but are not sufficient for presence to occur. In essence, presence in VR is about the internal psychological state of the VR user rather than the characteristics of the VR technology (both hardware and software). So, a VR experience may be immersive for one person but not for another, based on the presence of the person, which is individual and subjective.

Many other media offer immersion—indeed, it is the aim of media creators to create an experience in which the audience feels completely absorbed. The unique selling point (USP) of VR is that this feeling of fidelity with media is a part of the experience of VR. Mediums such as the cinema, television, music or the theatre all attempt to immerse and foster a sense of presence, but they are limited by the physical constraints of their mediums—a theatre cannot be a lived-in space forever; a television show will eventually end. VR, as a medium that projects a computer-generated environment, is limited by the constraints of the computational systems that it is built upon. VR *could* revolutionise immersion and presence, and this would be consistent with thinking on the medium—VR may re-engineer presence and immersion (Thrift, 2008: 95; Deleuze, 2005: 36).

Brown and Cairns (2004) describe the process of moving from immersion to presence as a hierarchical structure where a media user moves from engagement (committing some time and energy to the object) to engrossment (an emotional commitment to the object and less attention to other things in the environment) to total immersion or presence (complete cognitive and emotional commitment to the object). This model of immersion to presence is useful in contextualising the *Job Simulator* example at the beginning of this chapter. As one becomes more interested, amused and attentive to the tasks in the game, you forget the environment outside of the game environment and attend to the computer-generated environment as the primary area of attention. Quickly, you can achieve total immersion in the game thanks to the investment you make in the game itself. I have seen other players who can take it or leave it, unlike my partner who will happily spend hours in the game until the headset becomes too hot or the activity itself becomes tiring. Brown and Cairns's (2004) notion of a hierarchy of experience also develops on Milgram and Kishino's (1994) virtuality continuum, where the virtual environment itself is not responsible for immersion as a property of its existence but instead involves an engagement in a particular manner for immersion, presence and embodiment to arise from the virtual environment.

Explaining the Making of Immersion in VR

Immersion and presence are not necessarily concepts that lend themselves to empirical research. While the theoretical models and ideas outlined up to this point are useful in helping to understand these properties of VR in abstract, it is very difficult to concretise what these mean in practice. To attempt to do this constructively and to gain an insight into how these concepts are understood and deployed in VR, research fieldwork was conducted between August and December 2017 with VR designers, programmers and commercial managers in Brighton, UK. Brighton was chosen as a site of study because its community of VR makers, designers, programmers and advocates had coalesced around the Digital Catapult Immersive Lab (Hills-Duty, 2017). Eighteen Brighton-based VR professionals and 3 artists who were performing VR-based theatre installations in Brighton were interviewed. Seventeen male and 4 female professionals were interviewed, and by profession these individuals self-identified as 3 company directors, 2 artistic directors, 1 creative lead, 9 VR 'makers' or designers, 1 innovation manager, 1 development manager, 1 VR programmer, 2 marketing managers of VR companies, and 1 VR narrative designer. While interviews ranged in length from 20 minutes to 2 hours, the questions posed were identical and straightforward. Interviews were based around the core conceptual question, "What is immersion?", with an intention of being able to outline a series of views of professionals engaged in designing immersive experiences on what this concept means for them in practice. Following a macro-analysis of the data, a thematic analysis of the material (Joffe and Thompson, 2011: 211–215) identified five repeated immersive elements that reoccurred across interviews.

Following the criticisms of major companies in the last chapter, it is valid to ask why the designers and programmers working for those companies were not approached to contribute to this understanding of the key USP of VR. The answer to that is simple: the major digital economy companies were positioned as platforms that are aiming for dominance of VR as a medium, but the development of VR media texts (at least at this stage of the development life cycle) is being done by developers that are producing for these platforms, rather than the major companies themselves. Marshall McLuhan (1969: 53) argued that "media are not toys; they should not be in the hands of Mother Goose and Peter Pan executives. They can be entrusted only to new artists, because they are art forms". McLuhan was arguing that media as mediums are best used by creative individuals rather than companies, as there is a vision that goes beyond the exploitation of technology for capital in the use of mediums by such people. Therefore, this was an opportunity to understand how immersion is being made by engaging with practitioners who are actively involved in the process of creating VR rather than companies set on exploiting VR for extensions of their platforms.

Immersion, Conceptually

Immersion is a highly contested concept, which has a number of definitions and conceptual understandings from a number of fields (Bell et al., 2018: 2). Early theories on immersion as a concept relevant to media and media use focused on flow and optimal experience (Csikszentmihalyi, 1990) and on presence as an illusory construct of mediated experience not being mediated thanks to deep immersion (Lombard and Ditton, 1997). Rather than immersion being a fixed, definitive quality or qualia (as in mental state), Bortolussi and Dixon (2003: 37) emphasise that immersion is a hybrid, dynamic and interactive phenomenon that involves convergence and divergence to the state of immersion. Such a view emphasises the role of the individual in the construction of immersion, as immersion involves an orientation towards engagement with the media in question. Thon (2008: 33) positions this as a kind of attentional focus, a psychological immersive shift of attention that goes hand in hand with the construction of situational models of engagement (in this case with video games).

Ryan (2015: 73) furthers this notion of the psychological aspect of immersion by arguing that immersion is a kind of directed, intentional consciousness that relates to another world and reorganises the 'universe of being' around that world. This theoretical consideration of immersion draws attention to the concept of world as expressed earlier in this chapter: world is an existential locale that can be created through an existential nearness to an environment. In addition to these theoretical definitions of immersion, there are modality- or activity-specific instances of immersion: temporal, spatio-temporal and emotional immersion (Ryan, 2015: 93–106); ludic and social (Thon, 2008: 36–39); and perceptual-environmental immersion (Lombard and Ditton, 1997). These specific modes of immersion illustrate that immersion can be realised in different ways but also can be planned for in different ways. A game designer in VR may look to build ludic, emotional and perceptual-environmental immersion, whereas a 360° video maker will not look to leverage ludic immersion but can construct immersion through other means. Immersion cannot be thought of as a uniform, unvarying property or experience. The variations in immersion are contingent on individual differences in people and on the differences between intentionalities on the part of media makers and their design of media texts.

The VR makers interviewed showed some appreciation (indirectly) of the notion of immersion forwarded by Ryan (2015), in that immersion was conceptualised by some as involving a redirection of consciousness or conscious experience in another world:

> [Immersion is,] [y]eah, that complete sense of abandonment of the real world. You can basically get lost in this fictional world that someone else created, and forget that it's VR. Your brain disconnects completely.
>
> (Osian, designer)

The notion of brain disconnection here should not (obviously) be taken literally. The phenomenon described here is that abandonment of the real being and substitution of the real for the virtual and an immersion in another world that Ryan (2015) describes. Immersion as a detachment and replacement of the real with the virtual was expressed frequently in interviews as a heuristic for understanding the principle being worked with in the production of VR. Designers and makers of VR also frequently contextualised immersion in terms of what cannot be done or how immersion does not work. These definitions from the negative indicate that the quality of immersion is contingent on a process of testing, refinement and retesting rather than an instant quality of immersion in a VR experience. Osian details some of the issues with breaking immersion:

> I've always liked games because you can get lost in this world. If you sit at a computer for several hours, get lost in it . . . it's not the same as

moving around and feeling like the world is real. It's a bit more tangible when you're in VR. There's a lot of hurdles we have to overcome but I think it's by far the most immersive thing.

(Osian, designer)

The idea of being close to a more immersive breakthrough is important. This notion implies that current VR technology is not perfect in terms of what can be achieved through VR in terms of immersion. For consumer VR, this is important; the early consumer systems are providing an idea of the kind of immersion possible but not yet achievable. The notion that immersion is a hybrid and dynamic phenomenon that in itself is alterable to the maker and that the maker needs to reconsider continually is made by Denise, a visual design artist and VR maker:

So I'm evolving my sense of understanding of what the word immersion means because I wouldn't have thought that even a third person in a story would've been immersive, if you can embody the character in some way, but that's evolving now. Anything can take you out of immersion, for me it's like when I've lost position or tracking I suddenly go to a blank, pink or something, or if you hit the guardian zone or you're reminded that you're not in that space. I think full immersion would probably be that you can forget where you are.

(Denise, visual artist)

As these professionals work more with what is an emerging and developing medium (even for those working with it, never mind the consumer), their own understanding of immersion is changing, conceptually and in practice. The maintenance of immersion again is seen as critical in Denise's concept of immersion, and the challenge of maintaining deep immersion or fidelity is again an issue—here, in terms of design and technological issues. Immersion in VR is clearly contingent on design that maintains consistency or fidelity continua and reliable technology to deliver this continuity.

While VR was seen generally as a medium that affords new levels of immersion, there was also some scepticism regarding how exceptional VR is in the context of immersion:

There are so many things which are immersive. Listening to your headphones on the train is immersive, but it doesn't give the subject presence. We've got to be careful, because we're pretending to be objectively talking about the meaning of these words. All we're doing is constructing a consensus.

(Harry, VR programmer and designer)

David, a transmedia artist working with VR, illustrates this through a comparison of VR immersion with other media making:

> And that is because I don't see the headset itself as being immersive. Or you can make immersive content with the headset but if you think about immersion as something which takes over your whole life for a period of time like a PR campaign does or an advertising campaign which is targeted at you if you are their target of a particular campaign then that is immersive because then what that is actually doing is rebuilding your cognitive map of the world. And essentially creating a world for you to live in.
>
> (David, transmedia artist)

Sceptical interpretations of immersion in VR should not necessarily be read as saying that VR is hopeless for immersion. David's notion of the headset not being immersive is in line with the view of immersion given in this chapter. As a high-level, guiding concept for the design of VR immersion is a key concept, but in the context of consumer VR, there is clearly a trend to ground the practices of creating VR in knowledges and practices of making other media—an indication of the novelty of the medium, even for those making VR and especially for those consuming VR. The notion that VR is still new and is waiting for the model or method of creating 'true' immersion is commensurate with the development of the consumer medium—still early in the life cycle in terms of consumer media and still being perfected by those making experiences for VR.

Sight, Vision and Visual Design

The use of visual stimuli is obviously critical in VR, as an HMD operates as a form of sensory-replacement technology where the visual field is dominated by the VR HMD-generated visual environment. Steinicke (2016: viii) notes that the visual aspect of VR provides an immersive or semi-immersive experience through the creation of a place illusion and a plausibility illusion, contingent on the nature of the visuals. Blascovich and Bailenson (2012: 1) note that the brain often fails to differentiate between virtual experiences and real ones. For example, the patterns of neurons that fire when one watches a three-dimensional digital recreation of a supermodel are very similar—if not identical—to those that fire in the actual presence of a model. This tendency of the brain to be tricked into believing in the 'realness' of images underpins much of the design of VR experiences.

The replacement of the real with the computer-generated involves a trade-off between creating VR experiences and replicating reality (Jerald,

2015: 49). Our sense of familiarity with simulated environments increases as those environments approach reality, but only to a point. Indeed, if reality is approached but not achieved, then the immersive effect can be significantly diminished. The deterioration of experience from acceptance to rejection is known as the 'uncanny valley' (Mori, [1970] 2012). The idea of the 'uncanny valley' illustrates that attempting complete replications of reality may not be desirable as these can be rejected thanks to small differences between the real and the virtual. My immersion in *Job Simulator* was not thanks to the realism of the visuals. The visual aspect of that VR game provides representations of objects and environments that are identifiable as representative of everyday objects and situations. These are not perfect reproductions, but the similarity is such that I feel comfortable in that environment and immersed despite the clear differences. The visual design of VR can be thought of as a delicate balancing act: the need to have an environment that is contextually realistic enough to immerse people in the experience without being so realistic that people feel alienated from that environment because of the not-quite-right aspect of direct representation.

> I think sight is very heavily affected by the user in their imagination, so for some people it has to be as realistic as possible, we are not at this stage where we can do photorealistic, whereas others will quite happily accept a fairly low detail or point cloud type of thing or will even quite happily get lost in a fairly abstract looking world.
>
> (James, director of Immersive Technologies)

Again, it is important to note that sight or vision works with other immersive elements to create immersion, as James notes that dynamic writing is a critical aspect of immersion, along with visuals. Critically, photorealism is not seen as important because immersion can be achieved by being as realistic as possible. Kevin expands on this:

> If you're aiming to recreate reality you're going to fail. Until we've got a rendering pipeline that is as realistic as what we perceive in the human vision right now, don't even bother. We should make good of what we have, not necessarily ask it to do something it can't quite do yet.
>
> (Kevin, co-founder and creative lead of a
> VR/AR production company)

Realism and immersion based on realism therefore do not necessitate absolute realism in the eyes of an experienced creative VR programmer; just getting close enough to realism to avoid the uncanny valley is enough to create a sense of realism in the user. For a sense of realism that can assist immersion, a visual consistency is critical in creating a coherent VR experience that has a sense of experiential fidelity:

> So I think with visuals . . . you can get away with a lot if they all look in the same style. If you have a hyper-realistic world . . . these fantastic objects . . . and a cartoon prop as a gun . . . it breaks the immersion. Whereas if everything is like a cartoon prop it kind of fits together and it works. If you can keep things consistent, everything will fall into place.
>
> (Osian, designer)

Within this sense of consistency, opportunities are presented to VR makers to create experiences with a sense of economy that do not require painstakingly detailed visual work to render an experience that is super-realistic, as long as it is consistent and avoids immersion-breaking glitches:

> There's an awful lot that you can cut out of the experience visually and people still feel immersed, you can really play it down[. I]t can just be outlines and stuff[. I]t doesn't have to be uncanny or anything. Which is almost worse because then you're glitching like it's not quite right, then it's just completely not right but you can still feel like you're in this alternative reality.
>
> (Denise, visual artist)

This notion that keeping the visuals free of glitches, rather than hyperrealistic, is key to immersion was reiterated frequently:

> Visually if it becomes disjointed you immediately lose your sense of immersion. If you see glitches, your brain disconnects from the fact that this is real. Whereas you can avoid touch, because you don't necessarily need it half the time, but when you do interact with something and it doesn't feel right when you interact with something, again, the immersion's broken. If you have a really short audio clip that's looping, you pick up that loop—immediately breaks it. You need to blend all these things together and make sure you don't have one thing that kills the immersion. That's where the magic lies, perfectly blending all these things together so the users forget that they're in VR.
>
> (Osian, designer)

Consistency across all the immersive elements to ensure they are both in sync and free of glitches that break immersion are critical. The critical aspect of the visual in VR for immersion is to maintain a coherent, logical and consistent visual representation of the experience being presented—without this, immersion is impossible. Perceptual-environmental immersion (Lombard and Ditton, 1997) is contingent on consistency and avoiding immersion-breaking glitches rather than realism.

Sound and Audio

Beyond the visual, sound and audio were seen as critical in the interviews conducted. The immersive qualities of sound are well established; the role of diegetic (sound presented as originated from source within a media text) and extra-diegetic as immersive elements in cinema has been illustrated by Stam, Burgoyne, and Flitterman-Lewis (1992) and in the video games by Nacke et al. (2010). Garner (2018: 3) argues that VR sound needs to be understood as emergent in this way. Collins (2013) contends that the critical aspect of sound in immersion is a factor of kinosonic congruence against kinosonic incongruence. When sound is in sync with the other parts of the medium and organically originates from the medium itself, then it is more likely to contribute to immersion. Sound therefore needs to be made in conjunction with other immersive elements:

> I normally start with a concept image, and that's the baseline of the artistic way it should look. Then I take it to making some 3D aspects in models, getting the visuals right. Then I start worrying about character-player. . . . How we give them interactions, what they're doing. Then I start worrying about audio. The audio is the final bit, because player interactions and the way they move around can influence the way the sound needs to be. So if it's like a really fast-paced character movement then we can keep pace.
>
> (Osian, designer)

Sound also plays a role in locating the user within an experience, which is critically important in an entirely computer-generated environment:

> Audio is very important to provide that extra sense of being there and having positional audio when you are further [from] or nearer to something you would expect it to be louder, quieter, coming from the relevant direction.
>
> (James, director of Immersive Technologies)

Sound was seen as an important complementary immersive element. Without sound, some of the immersive effects being attempted could not be achieved. In VR, sound works in a kinosonically congruent manner, building immersion with other elements.

Touch and Haptics

Haptic interfaces in VR fit into a long history of tactile interfaces between humans and media (Parisi, 2018; Paterson, 2007), and discourses on VR have included notions of the importance of the virtualisation of touch and tactile realism since the early 1990s (Rheingold, 1991: 323). Haptic interfaces were seen as a potentially critical element in ludic (Thon, 2008: 36) and environmental immersion, but the ability of haptic interfaces to contribute to immersion is not, at present, seen as essential by all makers. This is thanks to two issues: firstly, immersion can be created without touch; and secondly, current interfaces for touch are less than perfect in consumer VR systems:

> Touch is probably the most important one, but of course it is the most difficult one because at the moment there is no easy way to represent the virtual with the physical sense, so when you are holding something you are aware you are holding a controller but you can be fooled into believing that controller handle is a gun handle, sword handle, or a screw driver.
>
> (James, director of Immersive Technologies)

For consumer VR to become popular on the basis of immersion, improving these haptic interfaces was seen as immensely important in the development of immersion in VR. Importantly, how hands and objects being held by hands in VR environments are represented and operationalised was seen as vital in creating a sense of immersion:

> I mean we have hands that are shown, we have big arguments whether it is better to show the virtual representation of the controllers themselves or have hands, controllers are better earlier on when you are trying to hand them to people but through talking with the developers at Oculus they believe showing their hands picking objects improves hand presence.
>
> (James, director of Immersive Technologies)

The imperfections in current haptic interfaces are therefore a potential immersion-breaking element, but haptic interfaces even in this form can improve immersion. The underpinning message is that we are still waiting for haptic technologies, just as the processing power for VR was waited for previously. As Parisi (2016: 166) notes, haptic interfaces have existed in a state of "perpetual immanence" across all media, awaited but not quite available. Perfecting haptic interfaces as a means of improving immersion is contingent upon technological advances that, as of 2017 and 2018, are not available but that may be available in the near future. Such was the importance of touch for many interviewees, this need for improvement could be seen as the next major hurdle to overcome for consumer VR. As current haptic interfaces in consumer VR systems like the Oculus Rift and HTC Vive are not perceived well, there is a tendency to look to the next generation of haptic interfaces to solve the problems of the current generation, while noting that controllers are (currently) a necessity:

> There are arguments for always having a controller, there's arguments for having no controllers and tracking hands. Tracking hands is a lot more natural and is a lot nicer, for doing natural gestures and interactions but then without the haptic feedback of holding something when you are then representing virtually holding something and you are not actually holding anything you get a disconnect.
>
> (James, director of Immersive Technologies)

Despite these issues, there was acknowledgement that touch is critical to immersion as the ability to manipulate objects and interact with objects, and things in virtual environments transforms perceptions of that environment:

> The more you tap into those senses, so for example with haptic and moving around and you can see your arm moving around and that's another thing of course, you see your arms more there and you feel more present within there. To really, truly make an immersion you need to play with all of them as much as possible (the senses), even touch. Once you do get to those type of . . . say if you push down on something and you can feel the pressure against it—that's when you start getting really immersed fully.
>
> (Nick, UX and sales manager for VR Company)

Being "really immersed fully" is the aim of VR in general and potentially of the USP of consumer VR, so achieving this is critically important. The power of haptic interfaces in immersion to create this level of immersion was most compellingly illustrated by David, when describing the effects and after-effects of haptic interfaces on lasting immersion in a VR experience:

> There was one where you are learning to be a barista and people kept putting their hand in the steam. And to me that was like, that is purely a matter of design. Because it would be easy. And I gave him an example of what I learned when I first got my Vive and I used it for 5 hours on the trot what I learned is that you cannot put things down on tables.

Because they are not there. So you know I had a hand controller on each hand and it gets uncomfortable every now and again and you do not want to do that so I kept wanting to put things on the VR tables in the VR world that did not exist. And then what I learned when I came out is when I reached for the kettle my hand kept retracting initially. I had learned that I was going to do it but it was not going to be there. So I stopped myself. So it demonstrated that it is actually possible for someone to learn to not put their hand in the steam.

(David, transmedia artist)

The learning described here is indicative of the kind of immersion VR designers want to create—a belief in an environment that is so intense, with such a level of fidelity, that it becomes a learned behaviour. David acclimatises himself to the VR environment through touch in this example (Parisi, Paterson, and Archer, 2017: 1513) and to such a degree that the touch behaviour learned in VR is persistent thanks to the habit. More importantly, the desire to use the surfaces of the virtual world as if they were physical surfaces indicates that the materiality of objects that can be manipulated through a haptic interface in VR becomes applied to other parts of the experience—the virtual is conceptualised as if it were real. After a hard shift at the café in *Job Simulator*, I've tried to lean on a surface and fallen to the ground too—that effect is real. That level of immersion, from the accounts given in these interviews, is rare because of the limitations of the current haptic interfaces in VR. More on that in the next chapter where the issues with haptics and touch as a barrier to the uptake of consumer VR will be discussed further.

Narrative and Story

Another key element identified in the assemblage of immersion was narrative as a source of emotional immersion (Ryan, 2015). Immersion needs a story that is internally consistent and logical, which the user can follow and is interested in. Narrative as an immersive element refers to the succession of events in a VR experience: the chronology (story), the verbal or visual representation (text) and the act of telling the story (narration) (Rimmon-Kenan, 2011). In this sense, VR is like virtually every other consumer medium:

Ok, the thing I'm trying to get across is the fact with a book, you can create the same immersion experiences you do with VR—if you do things with the story that don't actually fit because then they're not comfortable. If you're writing about a desert island you don't suddenly introduce a spaceship—then there's a different story, characters and tone because that would be immersion-breaking.

(Andy, director of VR company)

Consistency or fidelity continua were again seen as critical, and an inconsistent narrative could be an immersion-breaking factor like visual glitches or kinosonic incongruence. While VR offers the affordance to change and experiment with narrative, the most immersive narratives are currently seen as simple narratives:

In VR the framework is so new, the narratives that work best are the simplest ones, that take people on journeys that they understand and that is also what keeps people immersed.

(Andy, director of VR company)

Taking people on journeys that they understand implies heavily that immersion in VR requires a grounding in other, non-VR experiences that one can use as schematic models for understanding the environment the user is put into. As Ryan (2001: 14–15) states, for any text to be immersive, it needs to create a space to which the user can relate, and that space must have individuated objects that create the setting for potential narrative action. The use of simple narratives preserves the idea that users can relate to the narrative while drawing limits around the potential of narrative action. The views on narrative in VR expressed in the interviews may reflect the relative infancy of writing for the medium. As the medium matures, and the skills and practices of making experiences in the medium are developed, then narratives may become more complex and genre specific:

I am not saying that ultimately we will not be able to write for VR but I do not think we know what it is yet. And so by issuing all of those things and just being in that world and letting it suggest to me what it is, I feel like I am making VR rather than trying to try and make VR.

(David, transmedia artist)

David was drawing on experiences of writing for video games, theatre and other media texts and expressing that those past narrative experiences are directing his use of narrative in VR. There is still a major issue with how narrative may be written specifically for VR, what that process is and how such a process would be realised. For consumer VR, this poses a specific problem in that the experiences being produced for consumer VR platforms are not sufficiently differentiated from other media to resonate with the discourses of uniqueness and revolution about the medium. However, if people are immersed sufficiently by simple narratives in VR, this may not be an issue in this first wave of VR. If that wave is a success, then the development of VR-specific or native VR narratives may follow.

Mood and Attunement

The final element of immersion is difficult to conceptualise. Here, the term 'mood' is used, but 'focus', 'attunement' or 'orientation' could work just as well. What mood refers to is the psychological or phenomenological readiness for VR, an expectation that aids in immersion in the VR experience. The acknowledgement of mood is an acknowledgement that VR exists in a continuum between the real and the virtual (Milgram and Kishino, 1994), where our expectations and concepts of the virtual are partially formed before using VR. When using VR, we come to it with an expectation of what it will be like, even as a naïve user: the equipment, the idea of the visual field, the notion of the computational environment. In manipulating or shaping mood, this anticipation can be 'hacked' by the VR maker; some VR makers look to prime users to be ready for their experience.

> You prime people subconsciously. You prime people subconsciously in terms of description of the experience they're going to take, so with [a particular VR application] we had a tweet from somebody on a commuter train going to New York, and it just said "Thanks guys at [company], just used [application] on my daily commute into work, I now see the future". And for us that wasn't about the app it was about the fact that he understood that the app was going to take him away from where he was, because that's what people want VR to do—and we did it in a way that was seamless, that didn't involve him having to do anything more complicated than put the headset on.
>
> (Andy, director of VR company)

Andy describes how his application relies on an extensive foregrounding in terms of text (inside the application) that readies users to expect an experience, which is then delivered faithfully to them. While this seems obvious (and an extension of narrative), the technique of doing this is critical in the success of the application. This element of immersion acknowledges that VR use does not occur in a vacuum, and includes significant pre-conceptualising on the part of the media producer.

The Immersion Assemblage

These interviews revealed that immersion is a kind of craft involving a number of factors that must be skilfully combined to create the desired outcome. Immersion is therefore at the centre of a complex socio-technical assemblage, where different aspects or component parts of immersion in VR are not stable or fixed, but instead these elements can be replaced, displaced or changed. These elements are thoroughly entwined with one another in the production of immersion (Kitchin, 2014: 54). An assemblage theory view (Deleuze and Guattari, 1987) can provide a framework for understanding this complex phenomenon by emphasising that those elements are fluid and can be realised in multiple ways. In *Job Simulator*, I am immersed thanks to the created environment that includes sound, visuals and narratives, while I am also using the game interface to interact with objects and accomplish tasks. When using *Face your Fears* on the Oculus Go, I am a passive observer while perched precariously on a flimsy platform on top of a skyscraper feeling a genuine impression of height in VR, before I tumble all the way down. That is immersive in an intense, anxiety-provoking manner but has a very different assemblage of elements that can be part of immersion in VR at play.

Harman (2008: 370), discussing the assemblage theory of Manuel DeLanda, notes that assemblage can do things that would not happen without the elements that make up that assemblage. However, an assemblage may also have redundancy in that parts of the assemblage can disappear or leave the assemblage and the emergent effect may still occur. This model of an assemblage therefore allows for immersion to have potentially different elements of the immersion assemblage at play for different experiences. While this means there is no 'magic formula' for immersion in VR, there are tools in the developer's kit that can be combined to create an immersive experience that may be tailored to the kind of content being used in that experience. There are four criteria of an assemblage (Harman, 2010: 184) that can help conceptualise immersion as an assemblage. Firstly, an assemblage has retroactive effects on its own parts, in that the effect of the assemblage has an effect on how the parts of that assemblage operate. Secondly, an assemblage is characterised by redundant causation in that parts may become redundant or the assemblage itself may cause redundancy in some of the parts of the assemblage. Therefore, in an immersion assemblage, some parts may not contribute to the immersion. For example, the weight of the HMD is necessary for the immersive experience, but this may withdraw from circumspection during the immersive experience—we just don't notice that we are wearing a heavy HMD when immersed in a VR experience. Thirdly, the assemblage has causal power, in this instance to create the feeling of immersion. Finally, the assemblage has the ability to generate new parts and bring other elements into the assemblage. In the immersion assemblage, this would be an element that cannot be planned for in the design or programming of the experience such as the mood of the user to want immersion. This idea of matching expectation is critical to the experience of immersion, and this should not only be thought of as a perceptual issue but also as an orientation or preparedness issue on the part of the VR user.

Managing these different elements of the immersive assemblage is critical to creating immersion—a point argued a number of times by VR makers. The role of the user as a perceiving being that is assimilating the elements of an assemblage is made here by Andy:

> So, the first one would be visual, because you're playing with screens and lenses and things, the second; sound, the third being touch and interactivity. Now, the interesting thing about sound and vision is that although we think they're linked in our heads, the reality is that sound is interpreted much, much faster than the visual space and so sound is actually delayed in the brain to match-up with your perception of the world.
>
> (Andy, director of VR company)

Andy identifies that immersion involves the layering of different elements into a combined experience, and a critical element is the user who interprets these elements and is the site of immersion, as immersion rather than the other elements of the experience is felt by the user. This notion of building up an experience as immersive, with the user as a critical aspect of immersion, is built upon by Eric:

> I can start with the main example of [a VR experience that positions the user as an animal], which I think ticks so many boxes apart from what you are seeing here the intended way of showing, the installation was in a forest setting. And it started in gradual forest, obviously that is the whole pageant around it not just a headset and someone standing there, but the way we designed the helmets, the way we designed the path, the journey from the car to the car park, to the trail of the forest, planting certain objects on the way and then coming to this huge tree that you are seeing, and next thing you know someone helps you and puts you in a headset and you are seeing the same part of the forest just through the eyes of different animals in headsets. We can amplify that by using tactile elements such as the sub peg, that is vibration, that kind of arrests and vibrates and the sense obviously comes from the forest.
>
> (Eric, creative director of VR theatre company)

Each element in the immersive experience here is designed, tested and added in a sequential manner to build the immersion—including elements before putting a HMD on, which involve deliberation to create a perceptual frame for the experience prior to the start of the VR experience. This VR experience involves a crafting of immersion where the elements are not added sequentially but are blended throughout and are continually thought of in a kind of directed intentionality on the part of the creator to build immersion. The visual, the audio, the haptic or tactile, the feedback loops from vibration and the theatrical environment created as a setting for the VR experience are all involved in the creation, maintenance and development of immersion. Immersion, again seen as an emergent property of VR, comes through the blending and linkage of a number of immersive elements and hence fits the model of an assemblage as this complex phenomenon can be realised in a number of ways and modes (and so not discounting the types of immersion identified by Thon [2008] and Ryan [2015]) through the selection, development and experience of different aspects of an immersive assemblage.

As the 'revolutionary' aspect of VR, immersion plays a critical role in consumer VR. The implicit and often explicit marketing of the medium depends on immersion as a game-changing aspect of VR. What this chapter has shown is that there is no intrinsic immersion from VR; immersion is carefully constructed through the use of different elements that make up the VR experience. Crafting immersion is much like crafting immersion in any other medium: visuals, sound, narrative and the attitude or mood of the person experiencing VR all play a role in building immersion in VR, just like any other medium. Thanks to the infancy of the medium, there is no way of writing and designing for VR yet; makers have migrated from other mediums and bring the conventions of those mediums to VR. The genuinely new immersive element is touch, and while this does provide deep immersion in some cases, haptic interfaces in VR are still being developed and are far from perfect in consumer VR. While widely available commercial VR has now arrived, the ability to manipulate touch and haptic technology is still being perfected, which may put major limits on the immersive nature of consumer VR for the first few generations of the technology. This barrier to consumer VR will be discussed, along with other major barriers identified in these interviews, in the next chapter.

5   Barriers to Consumer VR

One of the unheralded benefits of talking to people is learning new things. This platitude may seem both obvious and ridiculous, but in the context of the re-emergence of VR as a commercial medium, the interviews based on immersion that were used in Chapter 4 yielded more than an idea of the concepts and practices of immersive design in VR. In asking about immersion, the VR makers were only too keen to identify what barriers they perceive in making immersive media available to consumers as justification for how immersion is a craft that can be affected by a number of contingencies. While the entire premise of this book has been that VR has arrived as a legitimate consumer medium that requires critical inspection, in 2018 there is still a sense of waiting for VR to take off. Discourses around the 'death of VR' (Lomas, 2017; Ackerman, 2018) with regard to the first wave of consumer VR systems (Oculus Rift, HTC Vive) abound in the technology press, thanks to the perceived slow uptake of consumer VR. This apparent demise of the medium has been exemplified in the failure of some major VR businesses, such as the closure of the VR start-up Upload in March 2018 thanks to a failure to secure new funding (Matney, 2018a). The death of VR was not predicted in the interviews for this research; what did concern VR makers were five key issues that were perceived as holding back the medium at present in terms of consumer impact. Revolutionary immersion might be possible, but without an audience there is no immersion at all.

The Materiality of VR

VR obviously is a medium that deals with the virtual, in terms of how the medium is a means to generate artificial, computer-generated environments. However, VR is also undoubtedly material. The HMD, the cables, the connections to computers or the connection to the unfathomably complex wires and servers of the Internet mean that VR always has a material aspect as well as a virtual aspect. Attending to the materiality of VR necessitates attending to the physicality of the medium. This is important because, as Miller (2015: 68) argues, developments such as VR mean that humans form assemblages (see the previous chapter) of embodied and extended cognition with technologies that "allow people to experience greater emotional and imaginative relations with media". The materiality of VR therefore is critical in understanding how the deep immersive relationship with VR is established and maintained. VR does not exist without the user, and that user has a body; we cannot be embodied in VR without being embodied in a physical body that is connected to the virtual through the HMD and other input devices. Hayles (2004: 72) argues that the materiality of media acts as a connective tissue joining the physical and mental, the artefact and the user. In a perfect VR experience, the body would be replicated in VR so our movements are replicated exactly in the virtual. The material aspect of VR therefore has a critical role in translating our bodies into the virtual in order to establish embodiment in VR. We are never a disembodied subjectivity inhabiting a virtual realm (Hayles, 2010: 379). Yet it is fair to say that this material aspect is still being perfected in consumer VR: large and heavy HMDs are gradually making way for lighter and more comfortable headsets; wireless connections are beginning to replace heavy and cumbersome cables that connect HMDs to computers or consoles; and stand-alone HMDs are allowing for a freedom of movement untethered from stationary computers. However, the materiality of VR as a tethered technology was identified as an annoyance:

> Yeah the wires are the things that really bug me. If anything I feel strangled by the wires. The tethering is something that I really hope goes away very fast. We are building on the assumption that we're not going to need those soon because they just strangle development, they strangle testing, they're awful. But that's interesting too as a restraint right, you've got this sense of like the umbilical cord, it's like the *Matrix*, you know, that kind of thing. But it's like you have to embrace that constraint and so, you know, what can we do with this constraint at any point? You can do that, right?
>
> (Denise, visual artist)

While makers are planning for a cable-cutting moment in VR (which arguably has arrived, although not with the high-end VR HMDs such as the Vive or Rift in 2018), the construction of VR experiences and applications currently are shaped by the physical connection of HMD to a computer/ console and the restrictions that this physical coupling places on movement, gesture and positioning while using VR. The inability of current-generation HMDs to allow for pass-through experiences, where the user can see the real world with a VR headset on (Alfredo, 2018), also means that the spaces that VR can be used within are largely defined by safety and familiarity even with a stand-alone headset. Material constraints are not limited to the headsets, though. As indicated in the previous chapter, haptic interfaces are also problematic with regard to barriers to the uptake of consumer VR. The limitations of haptic interfaces mean that the translation of the body and movement is very limited in consumer VR systems:

> Right now we don't track the whole body. So we track hands and heads and that allows us to make a semi-accurate estimation of what the player looks like; where they are in the world. They will never have . . . well they won't have legs—for now. Playing a game with friends you'll see a bunch of torsos and you can kind of get over that disconnect a little bit, but I do think you need the full person as they look in real life in that world. Which we can't do right now.
>
> (Osian, designer)

The prospect of immersion is implicitly challenged by the uncanniness of the body without legs in Osian's complaint about tracking the whole body. VR has been described as the medium in which interactive biological motion is emphasised (Lanier, 2017: 173), but embodied cognition, the idea that the body plays a role in cognition itself (Merleau-Ponty, 1962), will be difficult when the entire body is not tracked or represented in VR. Current technological fixes for this issue are not seen as being sufficient to address the problems with translating the body:

> There's a lot of shortcuts . . . for instance we could put a tracker on the hand, and we could put trackers on the feet but . . . you get a disconnect between the real-life presence and the virtual avatar and if they're moving across terrain and the terrain is slightly sloped up the character isn't going to be walking on a flat plane, they're going up. We need to solve full body avatars that look and react as the players are. I like to have full rig characters, I like to have tactile rigs on the chest and body as well, so for instance, if you get shot in a game you feel it. This technology exists but I haven't seen someone make a VR game with that stuff in.
>
> (Osian, designer)

The shortcuts and techniques for tracking the body that Osian details are ad hoc additions to the haptic interfaces bundled with commercial VR hardware, such as the HTC Vive Tracker or custom-built sensors. Even these cannot compensate for the difficulties that current haptic sensors have in terms of mapping and representing the body in VR. This creates some specific difficulties for co-presence in VR, the phenomenon of being in a VR space with other people. Having an accurate and responsive avatar is very important in the possibility and realisation of social networking in VR (see Chapter 6), which is a major current and future application of the medium (unsurprisingly, given some of the companies involved in VR). The inability to render the body and bodily movements, gestures and expressions accurately (while avoiding the uncanny valley) in VR currently is a major issue with the materiality of the medium. This is allied with a need to avoid cumbersome equipment that restricts movement, like current tactile rigs and many HMDs.

Interfaces

The haptic interfaces for VR are one issue, as are HMDs as a physical interface for the medium. The digital interfaces that one encounters when in VR were also seen as a potential barrier to the uptake of commercial VR thanks to their unsuitability to the medium:

> Unfortunately, because most of the people who come from a VR space come from traditional gaming or traditional menu-type systems, they try to shoe-in existing menus that exist on screens and computers. Which I don't think lends anything to the experience because you never see a floating wall of buttons in your life. It's intrusive and it automatically means it's not rooting somebody in the experience, it's reminding somebody that it's an invented space and that there's stuff going on outside that space.
>
> (Andy, director of VR company)

This issue is obviously related to the immersion-breaking factors identified in the previous chapter but is also related to a wider point about the development of VR experiences. The dominance of game-style interfaces within VR applications should be contextualised in the dominance of gaming as a cultural form in VR, but it also shows that VR has yet to develop a style of its own. The borrowing and adaption of other media into VR emphasise Jaron Lanier's argument that VR is the most centrally situated medium (Lanier, 2017: 54) in that VR is capable as a medium of absorbing aspects of other mediums at will. However, this argument about the unsuitability of gaming interfaces also echoes another Lanier argument (2017: 236) that VR designers should be fighting against things learned from gaming—even in designing games for VR. The overreliance on existing modes and forms of interface essentially prevents the development of VR-specific interfaces that would act to improve immersion as a part of the VR immersive assemblage—a set of heuristics deployed through habit and economy rather than as a result of their utility.

> The more you make something accessible, the more people will accept it as a functioning space. So, the kind of thing I'm talking about; the dialogue, the psychological biases, the fulfilling of the expectations that's been set, the ease of use, the access to different pathways to reinforce each other, all works really nicely in terms of rooting somebody in the experience. The problem with VR at the moment is that everyone is cutting at it—thinking they can take a game that's on a screen that's been specifically designed for a screen and screen experience and pop it into VR. Quite frankly it simply doesn't work.
>
> (Andy, director of VR company)

Andy's follow-up to the interfaces point amplifies this argument over the borrowing of features from other mediums. The adaptation of current forms into VR simply as a facsimile of their original form will not work and will not provide the kind of 'killer app' that consumer VR will need to attract consumers. It is not clear why a game made for screen media needs adaptation for VR firstly, and, secondly, it is not clear why such an adaptation would work in VR. Andy is criticising a laziness in the development of VR amongst developers (and major companies) where the shortcut to success is seen to be the provision of successful media texts in other mediums through VR, without a consideration for the unique qualities of VR as a medium. The wholesale borrowing and adaptation of existing media forms—without developing VR-specific forms that showcase the medium—is therefore a barrier to the provision of revolutionary and novel texts in VR.

Hype and the Language of VR

In the 1980s and 1990s, the hype around VR could not be matched by the technological reality of VR systems at that time. While the technological lag has now been bridged (albeit with the consequences for VR outlined in Chapter 3) there is still an issue with hype around the medium and the reality of the consumer experiences available.

> I think it's very easy to grab peoples' attention with it and easy to get people in—the harder part comes from getting that initial excitement to convert into actual sales.
>
> (Carrie, marketing manager for VR Company)

Carrie's role is to promote VR products and generate revenue from sales. While people are impressed with VR products, there is a reluctance to invest in VR hardware and software—not an unfamiliar problem encountered by interviewees across the research. Understanding this reluctance to indulge in the hype cycle of this wave of VR is more complex than just critiquing the project itself (and the product in question has realised significant sales). There is some indication that people are convinced that VR is only an extension of the games industry:

> But one of the key failures I would say over the past few years has been the overemphasis on the gaming market so if you look at 2014 onwards it has all been games, games, games and nothing else. And the mainstream press on board, all the platforms pushing their gaming elements but ultimately that has not been hugely successful.
>
> (James, director of Immersive Technologies)

These gaming discourses are inevitable in a way inasmuch as gaming and the cultures around gaming provide a language to contextualise and discuss VR in a way that makes sense. As Lanier (2017: 309) states, the root of the language problem in VR is that people are using 'old' language tools to describe a new technology, and when this is seen as a failure, then the medium itself is at risk of being seen as a failure. The problem, for Lanier, is that there is not yet a language of VR and that VR is indeed a language (Lanier, 2017: 222) that has not yet been 'translated'. Due to the lack of a VR language, the experiences and codes of VR are being translated into other language codes, such as gaming, in order to be articulated to an audience, without success. In a way, this argument echoes the argument of Lev Manovich (2001) on *The Language of New Media*. In that book, Manovich proposed a new language of terms and discourses that allowed for the articulation of key processes and cultural aspects of new media. There is not (yet) the same language of VR, which means that the hype of the medium is grounded in other media discourses that misrepresent the form of the medium and that communication about the medium is difficult without resort to familiar language on other media that do not articulate the benefits of VR.

> Exactly, because it's a language we need to develop, a whole new language, yeah and most of us don't know what that is I think and technical difficulties are still quite substantial.
>
> (Leon, artist and VR designer)

The difficulty in translating VR is not just an inability of understanding on the part of those outside VR, as Leon says. Those in the VR community also struggle to articulate VR in a language that can be used, and the technological aspects of VR may be a cause of this lack of articulation:

> I realised that when I talked about gaze interaction there was actually a lot of confusion just in that area that people do not understand that there is [sic] different type of gaze interactions and then as an academic I was like, there needs to be a discourse, a language created around that.
>
> (Rob, VR creator and academic)

Rob both designs in VR and writes about VR in an academic context, and while his work articulates the technological concepts of VR well in academia, this is not necessarily a form of discourse that will itself translate well to a non-academic audience. The need for a language to express these concepts not only to people outside of VR but also within VR communities is seen as an essential development. The aspect of communicating to non-VR-conversant people was seen as far more pressing by other interviewees, though:

> Do you think the people who commission you have any idea of what goes into making a genuinely immersive experience? They have a lack of knowledge. There's a lot of work there that needs to be done prior to doing pitches. And it's sort of simple things that to us in hindsight, looking back on, we have taken for granted.
>
> (Nick, UX and sales manager for VR Company)

Nick's role is to pitch for business with companies that have expressed interest in promoting their businesses with VR experiences. While he converses in discourses within his own business and with colleagues in VR who are technologically informed and mutually understood, the articulation of these terms to customers outside the VR world is difficult. Marketing VR therefore lacks a language of articulation. In the context of both commercial and consumer VR, this is important: if the makers of VR cannot articulate what people are getting from VR, it is unlikely that businesses may see the marketing potential and consumers the entertainment potential.

> People cannot say what it is and that is confusing people because I think there is a key thing of confusion with the terminology coming from marketing companies. To see something like that and then to create artworks that communicate the terminology used and have the capacity to inform practitioners across the board on these processes. I feel like that is part of what we would call the meta language of this new media.
>
> (Rob, VR creator and academic)

Rob expressly blames the marketing companies associated with VR for creating a misleading discourse or narrative around the medium that cannot accurately communicate the specificities of VR. The need for the language of VR is therefore critical in communicating the potential of VR accurately, as well as being able to inform practitioners about developments in VR not in their field. For a narrative designer in VR to understand the advances in lens technology, HMD resolution or graphics cards power, there needs to be a new, shared language of VR that does not borrow from other fields that have their own disciplines and practices of expertise. The need for a new language of VR is also acute with respect to communicating between the audience and VR makers:

> Now we're in VR, we now have that same gap between creator of content—giving a message the audience can decode, because there is very little shared language at the moment and very little understanding from the creator's point of view as to what the audience can actually take and understand. And the unfortunate thing I think about VR at the moment is that too many people are taking a medium such as a PC game, throwing it into this new space and expecting it to work, and actually people don't know how to consume. People don't like it—and because they don't like it, they don't buy it; if they don't buy it there's a gap in the market.
>
> (Andy, director of VR company)

Andy specifically criticises how the lack of a language of VR means that there is a disconnect between the maker and audience and how this is manifest in the creation of VR experiences that are not readily or easily understood by audiences—obviously, a major issue for consumer VR in creating an understanding of products for consumers. Nick articulates much the same argument with regard to business customers for VR:

> Yeah, I wouldn't say knowledge, but shared language between the end user and the creator. Because this media's starting to become more and more and more accessible, and more . . . people are starting to more use it, that shared context and information is starting to become more and more easy to understand between the both of them. But because it's still in that early phase . . . you've got to hold someone's hand through the process much as possible.
>
> (Nick, UX and sales manager for VR company)

Nick sees this issue as a problem of scale with regard to VR. While making promotional campaigns for companies involves a series of representational texts about that organisation targeted at specific audiences, VR as a medium involves far more than a traditional promotional campaign because of what VR requires in terms of designing an experience for an end user and how that experience is developed:

> I think that people need to understand that compared to other mediums like video and photography and print . . . you create that content; you might use fancy words, you might use fancy-cut scenes, you might have fancy effects on the image . . . but that is the amount you can go towards it to make it fluffy and nice. But for us, because we control the person's environment, absolutely everything they see and experience, that means you need to go through a load of different hoops and hurdles to make sure they have that experience—and add that fluffy-niceness to it. And that is a big sort of side that you would see in any other sort of medium—but it takes a lot longer, there are certain hoops you need to jump through and I think that's why not many people realise we are controlling the environment and the users around it. We need to create that in the correct way or people aren't going to enjoy it. As you say, otherwise you don't get that 'magic'.
>
> (Nick, UX and sales manager for VR company)

Making good and effective VR products for commercial clients involves more than the considerable task of making a VR experience, it also involves explaining the process and explaining how engagement and control are far greater factors in a campaign in VR than in any other media (even in the age of social media). To create something that has the 'magic', the language issue with VR must be overcome with careful translation and explanation to educate as well as to produce.

VR Sickness

One commonly cited barrier to using VR is virtual reality sickness, a phenomenon similar to motion sickness but without the need for self-motion. Brooks et al. (2010) argue that virtual reality sickness may be a major barrier to the use of VR, and the phenomenon has been termed 'cybersickness' (Lawson, 2014: 531), with a range of symptoms such as general discomfort, headaches, drowsiness and disorientation. Even for experienced VR users such as the developers and makers interviewed for this research, VR sickness is an uncomfortable phenomenon:

> So for instance I notice that when I spend too long on VR there are a bunch of effects, right, so one is just physical like my face feels

different because I've had the headset on, I see the world differently cause I'm used to looking in the different way it's almost like when you've got the magic mirror book thing, you have to use your eyes differently, so it's reconfiguring my brain to look differently so I then subsequently see the world a bit differently which is not a bad thing because I see the world in an interesting new way, my relationship to objects is different. But at home when I've taken the VR headset home a couple of times, the kids who are 9 and 12 spend quite a lot of time with it and my younger son spent quite a lot of time in *Minecraft* and then felt not quite himself for a little while after. There's almost like a hangover thing for VR and suspect that that's normal and we just have to evolve as humans if we're going to have VR in our lives.

(Denise, visual artist)

Denise's experiences of VR sickness are important in two ways. Firstly, evidence suggests that women are more susceptible to VR sickness than men (Munafo, Diedrick, and Stoffregen, 2016). A range of possible explanations are offered for this gender disparity, including women having a wider field of view than men (Park et al., 2006), which suggests that VR headsets and lenses in HMDs show a bias towards men at the design stage; hormonal differences between men and women (Kennedy et al., 1989); or gender differences in depth cue perception due to men favouring motion parallax (which is prioritised in VR) and women favouring shape-from-shading (Biocca, 1992; boyd, 2001, 2014). The idea that female users are more susceptible to VR sickness asks questions about the design and testing of VR systems in general and whether these systems are being designed for all or only for the 'most likely' to buy VR technology in the view of producers. If economic rationality is guiding design principles that disadvantage female VR users, then this barrier to VR use is coded into the design of systems and is therefore hugely significant.

Cost

Finally, the most common barrier identified to consumer VR was the cost of consumer VR systems. This is a direct barrier to VR; unlike VR sickness, which requires actually trying VR to experience discomfort or the issues with linguistic codes that make understanding the intentions of designers difficult, the cost of VR systems will prevent people from engaging with VR at any level. There are some affordable VR systems, of course. While smartphone-based mobile VR platforms such as Google Cardboard are positioned as affordable, these solutions still require an expensive smartphone being repositioned as a VR system. The launch in 2018 of stand-alone VR

HMDs, such as the Oculus Go, HTC Vive Focus and Lenovo Mirage, offer consumer VR systems for between £200 and £400, but in a crowded market for consumer electronic spending, this still represents an investment that many may not be prepared to make without a clear and obvious need for VR. The price of consumer VR was explicitly linked to the economic viability of the VR industry as a whole in interviews, with respondents clear that, without an economic base for consumer VR, costs are unlikely to decrease—but in a classic Catch-22 scenario without costs decreasing for consumer VR, this is unlikely to happen.

> I mean within the research area, like, it's all out making something fun right? Then when you make it commercial it becomes quite unviable. For a VR headset it's 3 . . . 400 quid. VR-ready computer, that's about a thousand, two thousand . . . then the chest piece itself would be about 2 . . . 300 quid. The mass market appeal is that £200 may be the cost but then they get a lot of content out of it. It's like with the console . . . not many people had a lot of consoles, so people relied on arcades to get their fix of consoles. I've seen that happen nowadays with VR, we're going into the area of arcades . . . we have VR arcades where we try out the VR experiences. And eventually the cost will come down and people will have this VR kit at home. That's when the fun stuff starts to happen because you'll have more developers working for it because it will have a wider mass market, more chance of getting revenue and more people wanting these experiences. Right now it's quite niche . . . it's more than niche, you won't really turn a decent profit on VR product right now. But if you do nail it, you're going to be there for winning when it does start to get more users.
>
> (Osian, designer)

The need for visibility of high-end VR through arcades is being recognised in the industry (Pattenden, 2018), and that development mirrors the early stages of the video game industry before console sophistication matched stand-alone gaming units and costs became acceptable to the consumer market. In order to get people interested enough in VR, there needs to be VR to use that will lead people into buying VR equipment, but with issues such as the linguistic codes of VR and VR sickness, this is still fraught with issues.

> All the enthusiasts from the next generation, I think they'll be disappointed. We'll need an economic push for another high-end headset. All the people who make software are interested in bringing price down.
>
> (Harry, VR programmer and designer)

This economic push for another high-end headset is an acknowledgement that current low-cost VR systems (which include the stand-alone headsets of 2018) do not provide the VR experience that designers are working for or that showcase VR at its optimal level. To make such a price cut in high-end VR possible, consumer interest in the medium needs to be driven.

> It is very much chicken and egg—if there is a bigger market place then it can support more content but you cannot get more content without a bigger market place. Or rather you cannot get the funding to make more content. Or a lower risk opportunity to at least break even but it is about patience and everyone talks about having to have patience with VR so early investor overhype—sorry, early analyst overhype and media overhype, the three contributing factors they all then turned around and at the end of 2016 proclaimed commercial VR when at the beginning they were saying, there was going to billions and then by end saying, oh it was not billions, it is a failure. Well, the only people saying it was billions was you so the failure is your predicament. But if you look at Facebook and Oculus they have been saying it is a ten-year game—it is a long game.
>
> (James, director of Immersive Technologies)

James outlines the cost predicament clearly. High-quality content is needed to push VR as a consumer medium, but with the market relatively small at this point in the re-emergence of VR, the likelihood of wide-scale investment in VR content is low. The large digital media companies see a long-term re-emergence of the medium that would see pricing of VR being adjusted over a far longer period than technology evangelists were predicting in 2016.

> I see the next five, six years. Facebook already made a huge investment in it and it's dropped the price down for the Oculus. So I imagine the next five years will have prices coming down to more reasonable point, maybe like eighty quid, fifty quid for a VR headset. So like a stand-alone VR kit. And then you'll have more developers going for it because more people will have the technology assisting it for revenue on return investment.
>
> (Osian, designer)

In order for VR to develop into a mass consumer medium, cost reduction needs to be mirrored by and to an extent powered by an increase in content development that would make VR an attractive consumer proposition. Long-term investment by major organisations makes this possible but not certain.

Overcoming the Barriers

The barriers to VR identified in this chapter are by no means insurmountable. Overcoming these barriers in nearly every case involves investment: investing in technology to solve hardware issues, which has already been seen in the consumer sphere with the Oculus Go; investing in development and content to improve interfaces; investing in research to solve VR sickness issues (especially regarding female users); and investing in reducing the cost of consumer VR systems. Investment is the solution to so many issues in life, though, and without a return on investment, there is unlikely to be the kind of investment identified here to resolve these issues in the short-term. The long-term approach to VR taken by Facebook/Oculus and others may see the phasing in of research, development and content creation that will see these barriers overcome, but this may be over a number of years. For the re-emergence of VR, this means that the medium may develop slowly and gradually rather than with an iPhone-esque immediate impact.

More pressingly, investment does not necessarily solve the issue of having a language of VR to communicate medium-critical concepts to commercial and consumer markets. Unless there is considerably more cultural impact than the medium has at present, a popular discourse of VR that conveys and accurately communicates the possibilities, affordances and benefits of VR is unlikely to develop in the short term. This lack of a language to 'talk VR' means that concepts in VR are continually grounded in other media—asking the question of why not just stick to that media instead of VR?—and that VR itself is not seen as revolutionary, despite the possibilities of the deep immersion, embodiment and presence that the medium offers. This can be solved only by increasing the points of discourse between VR designers and users through usage. Chapter 6 looks at what the current major cultural impact of VR is and how VR may make more of an impact to improve the cultural conditions for a language of VR.

6 Content and the Cultural Impact of Early Consumer VR

The previous two chapters sit aside one another like ying and yang. While VR makers argue that VR can provide a revolutionary form of deep immersion for users (as long as the elements are complementary and consistent to avoid breaking immersion), barriers still need to be overcome for consumer VR to fully realise the possibility of this deep immersion. The possibility of consumer VR being a revolutionary medium therefore sits in a dialectical relationship with a series of barriers to achieving that goal, and this continual oscillation between trying to immerse the user and battling against the constraints on immersion at present will have a shaping effect on consumer VR until the barriers to consumer VR are overcome. With this in mind, this chapter looks at the cultural impact of consumer VR in the first wave of consumer VR in order to critically assess what has been tried, what has worked, what has failed and what is required for consumer VR to realise the revolutionary potential of VR.

As this chapter is focused on consumer VR, the kinds of VR experience and genres covered in this chapter are obviously consumer in nature. This leads to an interesting omission, as arguably the most successful and immersive use of VR to date has been in a non-consumer context: training and education. There is no reason why learning to do something in VR would not be a consumer hit, but to date this has not been a feature of consumer VR. VR has had particularly strong impact in medical training (see Riener and Harders, 2012; McGrath et al., 2017; Westwood, Westwood, and Felländer-Tsai, 2016), training in military situations and simulations (see Seidel and Chatelier, 1997), architectural design training and implementation (Whyte and Nikolic, 2018), construction training (Sher et al., 2012) and other related education fields. Medical treatments in VR for post-traumatic stress disorder (Reger et al., 2016), eating disorders (Riva, 2017), mental health disorders (Freeman et al., 2017), stroke rehabilitation (Laver et al., 2015) and a number of other applications are also emerging as legitimate uses for VR technology with considerable impacts.

However, these are again not necessarily consumer applications; the focus here is on the use of VR as home media, where consumers 'consume' VR experiences as entertainment. As such, this chapter narrows the focus of the cultural impact of VR to impact on consumer media, with attention paid to three important consumer mediums that have been re-mediated into VR genres: video games, social networking and pornography. While Lanier (2017: 237) argues that VR is a new art form that must escape the clutches of gaming, cinema, traditional software, the new economic power structures and possibly the ideas of its pioneers, the key cultural impacts of VR in the early stages of commercial VR are re-mediations of existing mediums into VR. Bolter and Grusin (2000: 45) define re-mediation as the defining characteristic of all digital media, with the concept itself being akin to McLuhan's idea that the content of new media is always old media (McLuhan and McLuhan, 2007; Berry, 2013: 32). In this chapter, the drive to re-mediate old media is continually in tension with the need for VR to establish its own forms, an extension of the need to create a language and discourse of VR from the previous chapter; the re-mediation of other media into VR obscures the capabilities and potential cultural impact of VR as a medium.

Games and Gaming

An obvious place to begin a discussion of the cultural impact of consumer VR would be gaming, as arguably gaming is the most visible form of media reinterpreted by VR. The Sony PlayStation 4 is one of the most popular platforms for VR through the PSVR, and the Oculus Rift and HTC Vive are closely associated with games through the use of the Steam VR platform as a games distribution platform. VR should, in theory, aid the sense of presence in games for the player. Pimentel and Teixeira (1995: 15) explain that VR requires the same mental shift that happens when you become absorbed in playing a computer game.

Tamborini and Skalski (2006: 228) argue that VR technology enhances spatial presence in games by the game technology being able to match user expectations of bodily movement and orientation in a manner that playing on a screen cannot. For example, when a player in a VR game environment turns her head, there is an expectation to see the surrounding environment move accordingly. Therefore, VR incorporates bodily movement and orientation into the game environment, arguably improving the sense of 'being there' in the game. Empirical research on the effects of VR on user satisfaction in gaming is promising. Shelstad, Smith, and Chaparro (2017: 2072) found that VR gaming on the Oculus Rift enhanced perceptions of overall satisfaction, enjoyment and engrossment, creativity, sound and graphics quality in gamers. However, the depth of presence in a game environment would also be contingent on the immersion assemblage from Chapter 4— how the graphics, sound, narrative, interface and orientation of the user are harnessed in the game for immersion in order to lead to presence. So the success of games in VR in creating this increased sense of presence is not a function of the use of VR as a medium for the game but instead is a function of the design and immersive qualities of the game itself and the mood of the user towards orientation.

However, this necessity of user input into immersion should not be an impediment to VR being a medium in which gaming can see additional levels of depth and immersion in the gameplaying experience. Madsen (2016) argues that the commercialisation of VR has brought horror video games to the highest level of immersion and presence, generating more arousing mediated experiences in the genre. These findings are supported by Lin, Wu, and Tao (2017), who found that in participants who identified themselves as easily scared, playing a horror game (*The Brookhaven Experiment*) on the HTC Vive led to significantly greater enjoyment ratings compared with less predisposed participants. These players experienced more immersion, perceived enjoyment and perceived fear in the VR environment. This book began with the VR horror game *Resident Evil VII*, and horror gaming is one of the genres of video games that has been popular in consumer VR. The popularity of an already popular genre poses questions about the kind of games being developed for VR, though. On one hand, one can question whether the kinds of game being developed for VR—most popularly horror, first-person shooters, racing games and ports of existing big hit games—are the kinds of VR experience that will broaden the appeal of the medium. Indeed, having gaming as the most popular and visible generic media in VR can give an impression that VR is for gaming or at best is closely associated with gaming. While console and PC gaming command huge audiences and generate huge revenues, gaming as an activity is neither universally popular, nor is it the only application of VR that could attract attention.

On the other hand, gaming and the kinds of games popular in VR ask fundamental questions about the kind of investment and development being put into VR in its early consumer iteration. At the early stage of development of consumer VR, games can be divided into two kinds: VR ports, which are games developed for non-VR systems and converted into VR, and built-from-the-ground-up-for-VR games, games developed specifically for VR. In the former, Bethesda have led the way with conversions of major console and PC titles into VR: *Doom*, *Skyrim*, and *Fallout IV* have been converted to VR. Other successful ports have included *Superhot*, *Resident Evil VII* (with the VR version released simultaneously for PSVR) and a slew of games that have had additional VR expansions such as *Star Wars: Battlefield*, *The Last*

Guardian, Tekken 7 and *Wipeout Omega*. Popular built-from-the-ground-up games have included *Job Simulator, I Expect you to Die, Beat Saber* and many others. The difference between these is in the language of VR issue raised in the previous chapter. The built-from-the-ground-up games are considerably more original than the console ports; for example, *Beat Saber* is a VR rhythm game, where the goal is to slash light sabres to hit objects (the 'beats') in perfect rhythm with the music of the game. *Beat Saber* can be seen as an innovative game design with the immersive elements of vision, sound, touch and orientation working together to provide a unique experience. Games such as this can be seen as part of a developing language of VR that can emerge from the experimental tone of such games and the utilising of the unique features of VR (such as being able to mimic light sabres in the hand in a VR environment through haptic devices), where conventions of gaming are re-mediated and altered in the VR medium. The ported games take existing games and re-mediate the perspective from which they are played on the part of the gamer. This is not to underestimate the vast amount of effort and work that goes into the creation of such games, but the underlying logic and language of the game is created for another medium and transposed to VR.

Gaming in VR, at least at the early stages of consumer VR, is marked by a tension between existing and emerging gaming forms. This is a tension that runs through all of the generic uses of VR in this chapter, but it is useful in contextualising a particular stage of development of consumer VR. At the early stage of consumer VR, gaming sales are dominated by ported titles and some built-from-the-ground-up games. As designers and programmers work more (even exclusively) in the medium of VR, games may start to develop and extend a language and discourse of VR gaming. Brutal economics dictates that at the beginning, gamers need a hook to get into VR—and porting popular titles is a legitimate hook. Almost certainly, VR gaming will retain some of the conventions and features of non-VR gaming for the benefit of the medium too; the adaption of online gaming and co-gaming in the VR game *Rec Room* creates both a social and gaming space. Allied to the ability to create one's own games and gaming spaces and adopting other game forms such as *Fortnite* into *Rec Royale*, *Rec Room* provides a model of VR gaming as a social, shared and embodied experience that builds and augments console and PC shared gaming experiences. It is also free beyond the expenditure on the initial expenditure on equipment. While this on the surface appears like the kind of co-present, embodied gaming experience that should be ideal for illustrating the value of consumer VR, there are other issues with social gaming like *Rec Room* that are common to early social applications in general in VR and that are—to say the least—problematic.

Social Networking and Shared Spaces

The idea of co-presence with others in VR did not emerge with games like *Rec Room*. Writing about the ideas that informed VR development in the 1980s, Lanier (2017: 113) describes VR as a medium that can allow people, through technology, to become less isolated from one another, while avoiding today's social media replete with spying algorithms that organise and optimise people for the benefit of giant server businesses (Chapter 3 is a long discussion of this very phenomenon). VR and virtual environments as a shared space for interaction between people were seen as an important aspect of the VR experience, and clearly with Facebook buying Oculus, the notion of transporting social interaction from the real world and social networks to VR is seen currently as something worth pursuing. This has been pursued not only by Facebook; VR 'social media' applications such as Altspace and vTime predate the creation of Facebook Spaces in 2017. Indeed, Altspace was acquired by another major digital media company, Microsoft (Matney, 2017). There is a perceived value in the creation of spaces for co-presence and interaction in VR, clearly, and why would there not be? Facebook and Twitter are valued in the billions, with advertising revenue through the roof and a captive audience of hundreds of millions of people. A gold mine exists to be plundered if the social connections that have been leveraged in social media can be augmented with embodied presence in VR to create an even deeper, more immersive social experience than social media can provide.

The rationale for social interaction in VR has somewhat moved then, from a techno-utopian discourse of freedom and destruction of social isolation to a somewhat less optimistic re-mediation of social media in VR. This re-mediation process itself is far from perfect, though. Facebook's own head of social VR admitted that in its early iteration, Facebook Spaces had very little for users to do (Metz, 2018). At the early stages of consumer VR, social VR lacks the critical mass of users to make the replication of social media straightforward. When your personal *connections* are not using VR, your Facebook Spaces friends list may look a little sparse and not like somewhere you would want to 'hang out' socially or alone, as the case may be. The social options in VR are hence more like long forgotten hang-out spaces online (such as Habbo Hotel, Chatroulette, AOL chatrooms or even Google Hangouts) than the social networks defined by actual connections to other users. Sites such as Sansar (a VR equivalent of *Second Life*), VRChat and Altspace work as online meeting spaces where one converses with other users and can choose to create ties to those users or not, depending on the interaction experienced. Allied to anonymity not granted by Facebook, social networking in VR can appear a little like Twitter in that users can be contacted by and potentially harassed by anonymous individuals pursuing an agenda far removed from socialisation.

The culture of social networking in VR is troublesome because of this. Bailenson (2018: 201) cautions on the use of these applications, arguing that there is a need to keep an eye on how people behave in social virtual environments. Anonymity has made possible a "powerful subculture of Internet trolls who take delight in making other people miserable". While we are familiar with this on social networks, and there are reporting mechanisms available and blocks to put in place to limit such abuse, the embodied presence of VR spaces creates new issues that are not necessarily suited to the checks and balances of everyday social networking. As early as 2016, Jordan Belamire reported being groped in VR when using the social VR gaming application *QuiVr* on the HTC Vive (Belamire, 2016). While avatar bodies cannot physically hurt another avatar, the perceived physicality may carry a greater threat to a user than a tweet or comment (Bailenson, 2018: 202). The game designers responded to this situation with the solution of a personal bubble where other users can be excluded, but this solution requires some technical competency and proficiency to use, which may render it difficult to operationalise by the casual user (Outlaw and Duckles, 2017: 2).

The issue regarding sexual harassment in social VR goes further than the observation of a single user. When I first used *Rec Room* in 2017, I was amazed and appalled at the sexist and violent language used by other users, especially in the presence of female gamers and avatars identifying as female. While the experience of being in a virtual space with other people is fairly amazing, the misogyny and stupidity were more like 4Chan than a brave new world. These observations are not limited to my experience. Outlaw and Duckles (2017: 7–17) interviewed 13 female users of social VR and reported that these users felt very guarded in social VR environments, staying on the periphery of spaces rather than integrating fully to avoid potential harassment. Women in the study felt that women in general in social VR are singled out for unwanted attention in the form of flirting, experience a lack of respect for boundaries, are the recipients of unwanted socially undesirable behaviours (such as other users drawing giant penises in the Altspace drawing application) and had difficulty understanding and adapting to social norms in VR. Codes of conduct in applications such as Altspace and *Rec Room* were routinely ignored and did not prominently feature in the user experience. While the small sample size of this research may draw criticisms of the research being unrepresentative, these findings on user experience have been supported. Outlaw (2018) surveyed over 600 VR users and found that 36% of men and 49% of women reported experiencing sexual harassment while using social VR; 18% of men and 11% of women experienced violent threats; and 28% of men and 17% of women reported being targeted with homophobic comments. Social VR providers are aware of these issues, with the developer of VRChat stating that they are aware of and are tackling users that engage in disrespectful, harmful and inappropriate behaviour (Alexander, 2018) as such behaviour impacts on user experience across the board.

Social VR has an issue with harassment, which hardly makes it alone in terms of social networking. However, given the perceived importance of embodied co-presence in VR as a 'game-changing' feature of the medium, curbing and controlling such behaviour is a priority. Outlaw (2018) reports that blocking other users that harass in social VR is perceived as the most effective and preferable method of dealing with harassment, but it is arguable that leaving social VR and not entering again to avoid harassment may be the preferred option until social VR based on pre-existing connections takes off (if it ever does). As Rubin (2018: 122) argues, harassment of this kind is not only a crushing blow for inclusion and parity in VR, but it also represents an existential threat for the medium as a whole if one of the major benefits of VR cannot be realised because of the behaviour of users in VR. It is critical that developers and companies anticipate and pre-empt toxic user behaviours and provide tools for users to empower themselves and exercise control within social VR in order to shape environments in which they feel comfortable. Personal space bubbles that literally 'erase' avatars that get too close are one measure being used, but an automatic measure such as this removes control from the user experience rather than empowering users and avoids enforcement of community policies by erasing the issue. If social VR is to avoid the pitfalls of social networking—and realise the value obviously seen in the medium by the social networking giant Facebook—then addressing harassment before it becomes the defining characteristic of the culture of social VR is critical. In the infancy of consumer VR, there is still time to do this—whether it is done will be indicative of how seriously VR companies take inclusion and parity in the medium. If VR grows along the lines that Facebook and others anticipate and desire, then discussions of harassment in VR social spaces may seem passé as people turn to the kind of social networking characterised by Facebook on the Web and mobile-selected interactions with defined connections. However, as those of us who have ever expressed a contentious opinion on Twitter know, not all social networking is defined by such well-considered, safety-conscious relationships (indeed, not all Facebook connections can claim to be so careful), and the need to establish and maintain privacy and security in social VR is a major challenge that needs to be addressed if VR is ever to deepen social relationships as well as immersion.

Pornography

Like it or not, pornography is a significant part of the everyday interaction that many people have with digital media, and as a very specific form of televisual entertainment, it has unsurprisingly and very quickly appeared as a significant generic use of VR. Historically, pornography has been a significant driver of consumer media (Coopersmith, 1999), and so the emergence of pornography in VR and the popularity of pornography should come as no surprise. There is a danger of overemphasising the importance of pornography in the development of mediums (Coopersmith, 2006), but with the pornography aggregator site Pornhub reporting that VR porn videos hosted on their site receive 500,000 views per day in 2017 (Pinto, 2017), the traffic generated means that pornography demands attention as a way that VR has become a cultural medium. In June 2018, the SteamVR store began selling VR pornographic video games, despite controversy surrounding this decision (Cuthbertson, 2018), in acknowledgement of the potential commercial gains that come from pornographic experiences in VR. The emergence of the Oculus Go in May 2018 has been identified by key figures in the pornography industry as a 'game changer' for VR pornography, providing a major gateway to VR content and ostensibly placing Facebook as an unexpected ally of the pornography industry (Roettgers, 2018). From a medium perspective, VR pornography demands attention as again the potential for embodied presence and immersion provides a potentially revolutionary turn in the experience of pornography for users. The combination of VR immersion and teledildonic technology (technology for remote sex or remote masturbation where tactile sensations are communicated via a data link between participants) affords the possibility of a connected pornographic experience totally unavailable previously. Rubin (2018: 211–213) argues that VR pornography may be more human and less objectifying than conventional pornography. Rubin's argument outlines a reasoning that, thanks to the empathetic aspect of 'being there' in the scene, reduces the voyeuristic aspect of pornography, replacing this with a participatory intimacy that will increase empathy and decrease desensitisation and detachment with regard to the subject position of the viewer in comparison to the performer.

This positive argument for VR pornography is somewhat contingent upon the immersive experience supporting an intimacy and empathy that is considerable. This level of immersion may require a complete embodied experience, that is, teledildonics that allow for a sensory immersion in the scene that really creates a feeling of 'being there' through sensory biofeedback, as well and auditory and visual immersion. It is on this point that the pornography of the early consumer VR wave has issues with achieving the goal of empathy. Without teledildonic technology that would allow for the requisite levels of immersion and presence that can foster a sense of empathy for the performer, VR pornography is little more than a 360° video 'through the eyes' of one performer who is watching another performer. This is the kind of VR pornography being created by major pornography studios looking to capitalise on this new avenue for content distribution, not aiming for the use of technology like the Oculus Touch (even if this could provide the haptic feedback necessary for a realistic experience). The deeply troubling aspect of this is whose eyes you are asked to look through in this situation. Overwhelmingly, VR pornography forces the viewer into the subject position of a straight, white male (Allen, 2018; Rubin, 2018), and the experience of VR pornography is of a (more often than not) white female submitting to the sexual desires of the male actor. While occasionally a male version and a female version of the same scene may be made, the predominant mode of production of VR pornography is a straight and 'fixed' format (fixed in that the male performer is stationary while the female performer is the sole moving actor in the scene). This is very problematic as VR pornography of the kind commonly available at the outset of consumer VR is overwhelmingly an experience geared towards male desires and male subjectivities—although, this is an argument that could be made for the vast majority of mainstream pornography. The re-mediation of that aspect of the pornographic experience, the packaging of women's sexuality for men as Allen (2018) explains it, is the major issue with VR pornography as it creates a controlling male gaze that is arguably more powerful even than existing pornographic forms such as point-of-view pornography. The result of this is that VR pornography reproduces ideals around heteronormativity and hegemonic masculinity in eroticism (Wood, Wood, and Balaam, 2017), discourses that hardly utilise the potential of VR to alter the nature of pornography towards intimacy and empathy.

Due to these issues, VR pornography at the early stages of consumer VR replicates many existing issues with pornography, without altering the dynamics of the genre through technological innovation. The kind of intimate empathetic response that VR pornography might produce according to Rubin is contingent on further technological advances in haptic technology and teledildonics that would allow users to transcend voyeurism and the enforced (and maybe deliberate) male gaze into a co-present pornographic experience. As it is, this kind of pornographic revolution is in the near future rather than the early reality of consumer VR. Additionally, VR pornography of the 360° type is far from ideal apart from issues regarding the subjectivities enforced by the medium. Chin (2018) identifies that VR pornography requires the user to adopt an uncomfortable and unnatural viewing position in order to synchronise with the viewpoint given, that the ability to look around a room is entirely superfluous to the pornography viewing experience and that being unable to skip through scenes or fast forward to the 'action' means that VR pornography is a boring variation on the genre. Breslin (2018) even argues that VR pornography might be more alienating and less alluring than conventional pornography thanks to the uncanniness of the experience and the lack of feeling that the viewpoint afforded in VR pornography provides. VR pornography therefore might not even provide the kind of vicarious excitement that conventional computer-mediated pornography does, and with the addition of an HMD rather than using a smartphone, tablet or computer, VR pornography may not be the consumer VR driver that it was in the context of the videocassette or Internet. However, at the early stage, it would be foolish to reject the possibility of the kind of experience that Rubin (2018) believes VR pornography is capable of affording to users. Again, though, the early consumer VR systems may not be capable of delivering a truly VR pornographic experience, and what is delivered has issues that make the re-mediation of pornography an issue for concern in the medium.

The Empathy Machine

These VR re-mediations of existing media should not be thought of as an exhaustive list of the cultural impact that VR has made but as an indicative list of the key issues that consumer VR faces as it attempts to make a significant impact on the consumer media market. The major issue for VR as consumer systems become part of the crowded consumer digital media market is content that does not exemplify or demonstrate the possibilities of VR. The re-mediation of existing media into VR does not capture the possibilities of VR on which the discourses around the revolutionary nature of the medium are based. In Chapter 3, the gap between the technological imaginaries and discourses of the 1980s and 1990s and the realisation of consumer VR were described as a technological lag, where the original visions of the medium have been subverted by the digital media ecology and economy that have emerged in the meantime. In terms of that technological lag, the process may not be complete; there is still a distance to travel before consumer VR has the sophistication that allows content to move from re-mediation to original, VR content. In particular, the development of haptic interfaces and technologies (as argued in the previous chapter) are vital in transforming the experience in VR, as are developing and perfecting the mechanisms, environments and norms around co-presence in VR.

If the unique selling point of VR is an increase in immersion thanks to VR, then the key cultural discourse that is a product of immersion is empathy. The filmmaker Chris Milk advocated VR as "the ultimate empathy machine" in a TED talk in 2015. Milk suggested during that talk that, unlike any other medium he has tried producing content with in the past, VR allows people to connect "to other humans in a profound way" and has the "potential to actually change the world" in terms of emotional connections with other people (Milk, 2015). This idealistic vision of VR is a callback to some of the discourses on VR in the 1980s and 1990s, an example of a new narrative and discourse on VR's cyber-utopian potential and its ability to connect humans through immersive and networked virtual environments. Milk's emphasis on empathy creates a space for consumer VR (and other uses of VR) to adopt a positive social agenda, a marketing term to generate positive discourses around the medium as a cultural marker for VR. The current state of and problems with important cultural uses of VR indicate that the gap to realising the 'ultimate empathy machine' is fairly wide. Early consumer VR lacks the technological sophistication, appropriate content and sheer number of users to allow the empathetic vision to develop. Indeed, it could be that VR does not necessarily create empathy at all; Rubin (2018: 85–86) argues that in many cases, VR is aiming to create intimacy rather than empathy, although these may well complement one another as in the case of an idealised VR pornography experience (if such a thing is possible). Grant Bollmer argues that the term 'empathy machine' is a discursive formation deployed to legitimise an agenda for VR as valuable in terms of social interactions and social behaviours. Bollmer argues that "technologies intended to foster empathy merely presume to acknowledge the experience of another, but fail to do so in any meaningful way" (2017: 63). At the early stage of consumer VR, Bollmer undoubtedly makes a legitimate point. The possibility of a meaningful empathetic experience is limited by the content and technologies of consumer VR, making meaningful empathetic experiences difficult to design, promote and experience. The early cultural impact of consumer VR is, because of these limitations, distinctly limited. The final chapter of this book will address how this challenge might be met, as well as whether and when the full potential of consumer VR as an empathy machine and a medium for co-presence in media with others will be realised through the creation of VR media rather than re-mediation.

7 Conclusions and a Possible Future of Consumer VR

If this book has established nothing else, it is that consumer VR is here, and while that is exciting, there are also issues and hurdles for the medium to overcome before mass adoption. Just because that is the case, though, it does not mean it is here to stay or to become the dominant medium of our time. VR could go the way of 3D television, the Segway, Google Glass or even the Nintendo VirtualBoy and sink into obscurity without a critical mass of users and capital being invested into the medium. With the financial might of many of the world's biggest computing and media companies behind VR, there should be little chance of a contraction like that seen in the 1990s. However, early consumer VR has struggled for users and sales. The cost of 'authentic' VR has been prohibitive although this is less of an issue with the arrival of the Oculus Go and other stand-alone VR headsets. Far more importantly, the lack of a 'killer app' for VR has meant that the argument around immersion and VR being 'revolutionary' in terms of immersion has not penetrated the public consciousness because not enough people have been tempted to use the technology. So, while consumer VR is most definitely here it is here without an impact in wider culture and without the world-changing impact that discourses on the medium have promised.

In the introduction to this book, two questions were asked to frame the main argument in order to explore the impact of consumer VR. That argument was that, while the promise of VR as a medium with scope for immersion beyond other media is a revolutionary one, the politics and economics of VR follow many current debates within digital media that should call into question the revolutionary nature of VR as a consumer medium. Chapter 3 addressed the first question, "How has the emergence of a wider digital culture and economy impacted on VR as a medium?" Thanks to the technological lag of VR and the establishment of contemporary digital culture and economies, there is a danger that VR will become co-opted as a particularly powerful biometric scanning technology for data harvesting by companies whose primary business is data aggregation, processing and retail.

However, if one were to play devil's advocate, then the very presence of these companies in the VR space guarantees the future of the medium. These companies have invested billions into VR because they see VR as an extension of their business models, and, as such, the future of consumer VR is relatively assured in the short to medium term as they look for a return on investment and look to perfect the data accumulation possibilities of the new medium. On the one hand, this is great for consumer VR—more investment, better technology, more content. On the other hand, for those of us concerned with privacy and control of our data, there are issues to say the least. Whether who is investing in and developing VR has negatively impacted the arrival of consumer VR is debatable. What is not debatable is that VR sits within a crowded attention economy, and while the structure of VR is perfect for dominating attention, getting people to use it in the first instance is difficult. While major digital media companies can see the commercial and economic possibilities of VR, they are evidentially not prepared to stake entire empires on the success of the medium, instead seeing VR as part of a suite of technologies that contribute to core business practices.

The second question asked at the outset was, "What might VR achieve and how in terms of immersion?" This question has just as an ambiguous answer. There is, of course, the possibility of deep immersion through VR, but at the early stages of consumer VR, finding the right mix (or assemblage) of immersive elements is possible, but the barriers to this are considerable. Most importantly, finding the right haptic interface for deep immersion will need technological and design improvements. That process should be seen as rooted in a wider issue of the language of VR, where the lack of a common terminology and discourse for the medium means that the needs of consumers, designers, makers and technology companies are not connected in a comprehensible manner. Until that problem is solved, articulating issues with consumer VR will be difficult, and the product for consumer VR may be more re-mediation of existing media.

If that is the case, then the true capabilities of the medium will be masked by adaptation and imperfect rendering of existing media experiences into the headset. It is fairly clear that VR makers are still grappling with how consumer VR will achieve 'revolutionary' immersion albeit with a great deal of enthusiasm and belief in the medium, but until the issues of articulation and materialisation of VR are mastered, what VR may achieve is still an unknown. If this is just a problem of the product life cycle of consumer VR, then more technological refinement and development are needed to realise the revolutionary promise of VR in consumer form. While that may come through the product life cycle of the technology, there is no reason to suggest that it is a given for VR; this will require significant research and design to realise. Again, the presence of Facebook, Google and others may suggest that such technological refinements are around the corner, but if VR is conceptualised as a part of a wider platform economy by these companies, then technological improvements may be shaped by the needs of the company rather than by the needs of the consumer—a possibility of immersion just to drive data collection.

This seems a very sceptical and ultimately negative conclusion to the prospects of consumer VR, but VR is worth pursuing. When using a high-end HMD with touch controls, though, consumer VR is exhilarating. Like nothing else available in consumer media, the feeling of inhabiting a new space and interacting with a different world is exciting, exhilarating and alluring. The oddness and delightfulness of picking up a virtual object and throwing it just for the hell of it is wonderful. In early consumer VR, though, the sense of awe in doing this is short-lived and ultimately temporary. We get tired, we even get sick, and while some experiences are fantastic, few are world-changing. Yet it is strange that even after the long wait for consumer VR, we are *still waiting* for consumer VR despite having been moving towards the medium since Victorian times and having finally overcome the major technological issues that plagued VR 1.0 in the 1990s. VR may well be a medium that is always premature (Lanier, 2017: 204) but that also is like being in a lucid dream when it's right.

A Thought Experiment on the VR Metaverse

Those companies that are investing billions into VR are not pursuing a dream world, though, and a thought experiment that has already been largely conducted in a film by Steven Spielberg may map out where consumer VR may end up. If the near future of consumer VR is uncertain, the technological imaginary of VR continues to develop and take shape in the popular imagination. The idea of a VR world such as the OASIS VR environment from the 2018 film (and 2012 book) *Ready Player One* is an illustration of a VR metaverse, where an entire realm of human experience is created in VR, affording the possibility of existing in VR. In such a space, the user is so immersed in that experience that there is a feeling of being in a 'world' that is a VR experience. 'World' in this sense is an environment where one feels at home, an environment that makes sense, that has meaning and that humans spend time in as functioning human beings acting in an everyday manner. In *Ready Player One*, Wade Watts and his friends know one another in the VR environment despite never having met in 'real life'. These characters know one another thanks to interacting with one another through the affordances of the VR world they inhabit for much of their time and through being immersed in that world to the extent that the world itself feels like a place in which they and others are present, embodied and active and accept the OASIS as a boundless world of human activity.

Is such a metaverse possible with consumer VR? Conceptually, the medium of VR should be able to support such a vision. VR offers no physical constraints to the immersion and presence that can be constructed in a medium—VR can be built to any scale theoretically, even to that of an entire universe of human experience. Dodge and Kitchin (2002: 341) argued that geographical metaphors are often used to understand the spaces of VR but that such metaphors do not necessarily limit how VR spaces may be designed; indeed, VR spaces being contradictory to everyday understandings of physical space are possible (Mitchell, 1995: 8–9). Holtzman (1994: 210) described the makers of VR spaces as 'space makers' in the sense that new forms of space are made in VR, while arguing that the kinds of spaces made in this process are themselves anti-spatial in that the rules and laws of space and spatiality can be ignored in VR. So any spaces made in VR that possess geographical qualities do so only because they have been designed and implemented that way—and therefore could be planetary in scale. The same goes for time (Ash, 2015: 213) as, in a cyberspace, there is no time in the sense that we have time in the everyday world—there are only processes of spacing and timing through the interface used. A VR 'cyberspace' or metaverse can be distanceless and timeless until it is designed to have distance and time through the process of design. In principle, VR should afford the possibilities of a computationally designed universe with its own laws, just like the OASIS.

The notion of the metaverse, however, asks fundamental questions of our relationship to media. Ostensibly, such a world would require the total re-engineering of presence. Presence as a phenomenon is very closely related intricately to existence, being, knowledge, representation and nothingness (Nancy, 1993) and so would be critical in a metaverse for more than just an embodied presence. However, our presence in everyday life, or the 'real' world, should be differentiated from telepresence or virtual presence in VR. Everyday presence involves a connection with the immediate environment. Telepresence is a feeling of presence with objects (physical or virtual) that are located elsewhere, and virtual presence refers to the same feeling with computer-generated objects (Sheridan, 1992, in Garner, 2018: 87). To turn telepresence in VR into worldly presence would require a reorientation to the VR experience through the mood of the user (Evans, 2015: 49) to accept the VR world as a 'world', in that the end result of a high degree of immersion and presence through VR would be a sense of 'worldhood' (Heidegger, 1962; Evans, 2015: 43–44). Worldhood is the relational involvement that we have to things in the world and how we stand in relation to those things in the world as a being who understands the world (Evans, 2015: 43–44).

Put simply, world is an existential locale—it is a place that we understand and are comfortable 'living in' or dwelling within—existing. Presence is often related to place; Slater (2009) argues that presence is the qualia (or internal quality) of having the sensation of being in a real place. World would be an extension of that qualia across a VR experience. Should VR end up creating a 'world', then this would be a VR experience where the user is immersed, feels presence and has a meaningful relationship to other entities and objects in that 'world'—just the kind of experience that discourses on the exceptionalness of VR extol.

So if VR can create a 'world' for us in this way, then the experience of being in that world becomes important. The phrase 'being-in' is chosen deliberately because it draws upon the work of the German phenomenologist Martin Heidegger (1962, 2008). Heidegger's work on world and place (see Evans, 2015: 60–65) draws attention to how our manner of being in a place leads to a familiarity with that place. Heidegger calls this mood or attunement to place 'dwelling' (Heidegger, 2008: 247), and in this view we dwell by attuning ourselves to a local world through our activity and orientation to that locale that eradicates the phenomenological distance that we feel to the unfamiliar. We dwell by being concerned about things and other entities in a place—we take these things into *care* (Heidegger, 1962: 244), and this creates a kind of nearness to things that allows a sense of dwelling (Malpas, 2000: 218) in an environment to develop. In a VR experience of total immersion or presence, the nearness to that environment is created through the different elements of the VR experience (immersion) and the mood or orientation of the user towards the environment (presence) to create a sense of dwelling or comfort in the VR environment that would be akin to dwelling in a world. This kind of orientation or mood is part of the immersion assemblage of Chapter 4, and in realising a metaverse, such an orientation would need to be totalising; that is, that feeling of being oriented towards the VR world would have to be present at all times. While a metaverse is not 'real', it is a world thanks to the orientation of the users to that place; it is a meaningful locale (i.e., meaningful activities occur 'there') that people can exist within and accept that existence as meaningful and everyday. Graham and Zook (2011: 131) call this phenomena 'digiplace', a place or sense of place that emerges from the influence of cyberspace itself. So if VR can be built to a requisite scale and if haptic technology and interpersonal interfaces in VR can be improved so that we can develop care, in theory the metaverse is possible—just maybe not desirable.

The goal of consumer VR may not be, at the very early stages, to make worlds on the scale of the OASIS, but the promise of VR is to create this kind of metaverse or world where people can exist, as opposed to the temporary and transient immersion and presence felt through re-mediation of other media. That VR may be able to create worlds; entirely computer-generated worlds no less is the essence of the revolutionary nature of the medium. This desire to make new worlds is not in itself a new horizon of human endeavour. Gray (2016: 14) argues that humans are always in a position of trying to make themselves the masters of nature. VR offers an opportunity to do this as a new reality will entail a new nature and new rules of science that can be dictated by man rather than followed by man. When thinking of the character of a potential VR world, then the politics and ideologies of the makers of that world will be as important as the technological possibility of the world. As Krämer (2006: 94) notes, VR itself is an extension of the attempts to store and produce physical realities themselves across all technological media. If VR lives up to its promise, then this may be achieved with the result being that physical realities now have an alternative option—and this is where the serious questions should kick in. The possibility of 'living in' the Facebook/Oculus metaverse or the Google VRWorld should lead to inevitable questions about what kind of world that would be like. At worst, that life would constitute being a hyperrealised data subject, surveilled continually and subjected to continual targeted information and behavioural nudges. That vision brings to life Lanier's (2017) concern about the 'digital Skinner Box' where our every movement and gesture is manipulated and measured in the pursuit of data and the commoditisation of everyday life. Virilio (2008: 45) sees that possibility as a kind of stereoscopic existence, where touch is replaced by touch technologies, optics are replaced by electro-optics and no difference exists between the virtual and the real—a mingling and interchangeability of the virtual and real. VR would be so integrated into everyday life and everyday experience that the difference between real and virtual is erased because of the quality of presence and immersion in VR. Potentially the worst of the modernist drive to remake humanity and the world in a technological form that keeps the user satisfied and content at all times—the stuff of sci-fi horror.

Fortunately, consumer VR is far away from the metaverse and needs significant improvements technologically and in terms of user experience before such a vision could begin to be implemented. Fundamentally, VR today is delivered via an app store model that became popular with mobile computing but would not be the way for companies to deploy at mass scale and push updates such as a metaverse would require. A webVR model would allow for a network effect that a metaverse would require, but the technological affordances of the Web are not attuned to the needs of VR (for now). Facebook's vision for VR is for one billion people to be in VR; if consumer VR ever gets close to that, then these questions about the metaverse and whether we want it would be asked far too late. It would also mean consumer VR was not just here—it would have won.

Bibliography

Abi-Heila, G. (2018). Attention hacking is the epidemic of our generation . . . *Hackernoon*. Retrieved March 01, 2018, from https://hackernoon.com/attention-hacking-is-the-epidemic-of-our-generation-e212e111c675

Ackerman, D. (2018). It's time to break up with VR. *CNet*. Retrieved April 03, 2018, from www.cnet.com/news/its-time-to-break-up-with-vr/

Alexander, J. (2018). VRChat team speaks up on player harassment in open letter. *Polygon*. Retrieved January 10, 2018, from www.polygon.com/2018/1/10/16875716/vrchat-safety-concerns-open-letter-players-behavior

Alfredo. (2018). The case for passthrough with VR. *Medium*. Retrieved April 01, 2018, from https://medium.com/@alfredos/the-case-for-passthrough-with-vr-a620b26e42bb

Allen, C. (2018). How to build the world's biggest VR website: Pivot to hardcore porn. *Wired UK*. Retrieved March 19, 2018, from www.wired.co.uk/article/vr-porn-360-pornhub-vr-video

Artaud, A. (1958). *The Theatre and Its Double* (M. C. Richards, Trans.). New York: Grove Weidenfeld.

Ash, J. (2015). *The Interface Envelope: Gaming and the Logics of Affective Design*. New York: Bloomsbury Academic.

Bailenson, J. (2018). *Experience on Demand: What Virtual Reality Is, How It Works, and What It Can Do*. New York: W.W. Norton & Company.

Barbrook, R., & Cameron, A. (1996). The Californian ideology. *Science as Culture*, *6* (1), pp. 44–72. doi:10.1080/09505439609526455

Barlow, J. P. (1996). *A Declaration of the Independence of Cyberspace*. Retrieved February 24, 2018, from www.eff.org/cyberspace-independence

Batchen, G. (1998). Spectres of cyberspace. In N. Mirzeoff (Ed.), *The Visual Culture Reader* (pp. 237–242). New York: Routledge.

Baudrillard, J. (1990). *Seduction*. Montreal: New World Perspectives.

Baudrillard, J. (2009). *The Gulf War Did Not Take Place*. Sydney: Power.

Baudrillard, J. (2014). *Simulacra and Simulation* (S. F. Glaser, Trans.). Ann Arbor: University of Michigan Press.

Baudrillard, J. (2017). *The Consumer Society: Myths and Structures* (G. Ritzer & B. Smart, Trans.). Los Angeles: Sage.

Becker, G. S. (1965). A theory of the allocation of time. *The Economic Journal, 75* (299), pp. 493–517. doi:10.2307/2228949

Beer, D. (2015). Productive measures: Culture and measurement in the context of everyday neoliberalism. *Big Data & Society, 2* (1), pp. 1–13. doi:10.1177/2053951715578951

Belamire, J. (2016). *My First Virtual Reality Groping—Athena Talks—Medium.* Retrieved February 01, 2018, from https://medium.com/athena-talks/my-first-virtual-reality-sexual-assault-2330410b62ee

Bell, A., Ensslin, A., Van Der Bom, I., & Smith, J. (2018). Immersion in digital fiction. *International Journal of Literary Linguistics, 7* (1), pp. 1–22. doi:10.15462/ijll.v7i1.105

Berners-Lee, T. (2018). The web can be weaponised—and we can't count on big tech to stop it. *The Guardian.* Retrieved March 15, 2018, from www.theguardian.com/commentisfree/2018/mar/12/tim-berners-lee-web-weapon-regulation-open-letter

Berry, D. M. (2011). *The Philosophy of Software: Code and Mediation in the Digital Age.* Basingstoke: Palgrave Macmillan.

Berry, D. M. (2013). Against remediation. In G. Lovink & M. Rasch (Eds.), *Unlike Us: Social Media Monopolies and Their Alternatives* (pp. 31–49). Amsterdam: Institute for Network Cultures.

Biocca, F. (1992). Will simulation sickness slow down the diffusion of virtual environment technology? *Presence: Teleoperators and Virtual Environments, 1* (3), pp. 334–343. doi:10.1162/pres.1992.1.3.334

Blascovich, J., & Bailenson, J. (2012). *Infinite Reality: The Hidden Blueprint of Our Virtual Lives.* New York: Harper Collins.

Bollmer, G. (2017). Empathy machines. *Media International Australia, 165* (1), pp. 63–76. doi:10.1177/1329878x17726794

Bolter, J. D., & Grusin, R. (2000). *Remediation: Understanding New Media.* Cambridge, MA: MIT Press.

Bortolussi, M., & Dixon, P. (2003). *Psychonarratology: Foundations for the Empirical Study of Literary Response.* Cambridge: Cambridge University Press.

Bowman, D. A., & McMahan, R. P. (2007). Virtual reality: How much immersion is enough? *Computer, 40* (7), pp. 36–43. doi:10.1109/mc.2007.257

boyd, d. (2001). *Depth Cues in Virtual Reality and the Real World: Understanding Differences in Depth Perception by Studying Shape-from-Shading and Motion Parallax.* Unpublished undergraduate dissertation, Providence, RI: Brown University.

boyd, d. (2014). Is the Oculus Rift sexist? (plus response to criticism). *Zephoria.* Retrieved February 1, 2018, from www.zephoria.org/thoughts/archives/2014/04/03/is-the-oculus-rift-sexist.html

Bratton, B. H. (2016). *The Stack—On Software and Sovereignty.* Cambridge, MA: MIT Press.

Breslin, S. (2018). Porn's Uncanny Valley. *The Atlantic.* Retrieved June 01, 2018, from www.theatlantic.com/amp/article/561521

Brooks, J. O., Goodenough, R. R., Crisler, M. C., Klein, N. D., Alley, R. L., Koon, B. L., & Wills, R. F. (2010). Simulator sickness during driving simulation studies. *Accident Analysis & Prevention, 42* (3), pp. 788–796. doi:10.1016/j.aap. 2009.04.013

Brown, E., & Cairns, P. (2004). A grounded investigation of game immersion. *Extended Abstracts of the 2004 Conference on Human Factors and Computing Systems—CHI 04.* doi:10.1145/985921.986048. Retrieved August 24, 2018, from http://complexworld.pbworks.com/f/Brown+and+Cairns+(2004).pdf

Burbules, N. C., Nolan, J., Hunsinger, J., & Trifonas, P. (2006). Rethinking the virtual. In J. Weiss (Ed.), *The International Handbook of Virtual Learning Environments* (pp. 37–58). Dordrecht: Springer.

Bye, K. (2018). #641: Oculus' Privacy Architects on their Open-Ended Privacy Policy & Biometric Data. *Voices of VR Podcast.* Retrieved April 20, 2018, from http://voicesofvr.com/461-oculus-privacy-architects-on-their-open-ended-privacy-policy-biometric-data/

Cadwalladr, C., & Graham-Harrison, E. (2018). How Cambridge Analytica turned Facebook 'likes' into a lucrative political tool. *The Guardian.* Retrieved March 17, 2018, from www.theguardian.com/technology/2018/mar/17/facebook-cambridge-analytica-kogan-data-algorithm

Cameron, A. (1995). Dissimulations. *Mute, Digital Art Critique, 1.*

Capcom. (2018). *Global Stats.* Retrieved February 06, 2018, from www.residentevil. net/en/sevenrecord.html

Carr, N. G. (2014). *The Glass Cage: Automation and Us.* New York: W.W. Norton & Company.

Castells, M. (1996). *The Rise of the Network Society.* Oxford: Blackwell.

Castronova, E. (2005). *Synthetic Worlds: The Business and Culture of Online Games.* Chicago: University of Chicago Press.

Chandler, D. (1994). *The Transmission Model of Communication.* Retrieved February 22, 2018, from http://visual-memory.co.uk/daniel/Documents/short/trans.html

Chang, E. (2018). *Brotopia: Breaking Up the Boys Club of Silicon Valley.* New York: Portfolio/Penguin.

Chesher, C. (1994). Colonizing virtual reality. *Cultronix, 1,* 15–28.

Chin, M. (2018). VR porn will never take off until it solves these 3 problems. *Mashable.* Retrieved May 16, 2018, from https://mashable.com/2018/05/16/vr-porn-problems

Chun, W. (2011). *Programmed Visions Software and Memory.* Cambridge, MA: MIT Press.

Collins, K. (2013). *Playing with Sound: A Theory of Interacting with Sound and Music in Video Games.* Cambridge, MA: MIT Press.

Comment, B. (2003). *The Panorama.* London: Reaktion.

Coopersmith, J. (1999). The role of the pornography industry in the development of videotape and the Internet. *1999 International Symposium on Technology and Society—Women and Technology: Historical, Societal, and Professional Perspectives. Proceedings. Networking the World (Cat. No.99CH37005).* doi:10.1109/istas.1999.787327

Coopersmith, J. (2006). Does your mother know what YouReallyDo? The changing nature and image of computer-based pornography. *History and Technology, 22* (1), pp. 1–25. doi:10.1080/07341510500508610

Csikszentmihalyi, M. (1990). *Flow: The Psychology of Optimal Experience.* New York: Harper Row.

Cuthbertson, A. (2018). VR porn games will be sold on Steam in 'jaw-dropping' decision. *The Independent.* Retrieved June 07, 2018, from www.independent.co.uk/life-style/gadgets-and-tech/news/steam-store-vr-porn-virtual-reality-valve-video-games-a8387331.html

Davis, M. H., Conklin, L., Smith, A., & Luce, C. (1996). Effect of perspective taking on the cognitive representation of persons: A merging of self and other. *Journal of Personality and Social Psychology, 70* (4), pp. 713–726. doi:10.1037//0022–3514.70.4.713

Debord, G. (1977). *Society of the Spectacle.* Detroit: Black & Red.

Deleuze, G. (2005). *Francis Bacon: The Logic of Sensation.* London: Continuum.

Deleuze, G., & Guattari, F. (1987). *A Thousand Plateaus: Capitalism and Schizophrenia* (B. Massumi, Trans.). Minneapolis: University of Minnesota Press.

Dodge, M., & Kitchin, R. (2002). There's no there there. In P. Fisher & D. Unwin (Eds.), *Virtual Reality in Geography* (pp. 341–361). London: Taylor and Francis.

Earnshaw, R. A., Gigante, M. A., & Jones, H. (1994). *Virtual Reality Systems.* San Diego, CA: Academic Press.

Elden, S. (2003). Taking the measure of the Beiträge. *European Journal of Political Theory, 2* (1), pp. 35–56. doi:10.1177/1474885103002001278

Engler, C. E. (1992). Affordable VR by 1994. *Computer Gaming World.* Retrieved January 07, 2018, from www.cgwmuseum.org/galleries/index.php?year=1992&pub=2&id=100

Evans, L. (2015). *Locative Social Media: Place in the Digital Age.* Basingstoke: Palgrave Macmillan.

Feltham, J. (2018). Nvidia Predicts 50 Million VR Headsets Sold By 2021. *Upload VR.* Retrieved January 30, 2018, from https://uploadvr.com/nvidia-predicts-50-million-vr-headsets-sold-2021/

Floridi, L. (2015). The present and foreseeable future of artificial intelligence. In F. Sabba (Ed.), *Noetica versus informatica: Le nuove strutture della comunicazione scientifica* (pp. 131–136). Florence: Olschki.

Foley, J. D. (1987). Interfaces for advanced computing. *Scientific American, 257* (4), pp. 126–135. Retrieved January 30, 2018.

Foucault, M. (1977). *Discipline and Punish: The Birth of the Prison* (A. Sheridan, Trans.). London: Penguin Books.

Fox, J., Arena, D., & Bailenson, J. N. (2009). Virtual reality. *Journal of Media Psychology, 21* (3), pp. 95–113. doi:10.1027/1864–1105.21.3.95

Freeman, D., Reeve, S., Robinson, A., Ehlers, A., Clark, D., Spanlang, B., & Slater, M. (2017). Virtual reality in the assessment, understanding, and treatment of mental health disorders. *Psychological Medicine, 47* (14), pp. 2393–2400. doi:10.1017/s003329171700040x

Fuchs, C. (2008). *Internet and Society: Social Theory in the Information Age.* New York: Routledge.

Fuchs, C. (2010). Labor in informational capitalism and on the internet. *The Information Society, 26* (3), 179–196.

Fuchs, C. (2011). Critique of the political economy of Web 2.0 surveillance. In C. Fuchs, K. Boersma, A. Albrechtslund, & M. Sandoval (Eds.), *Internet and Surveillance: The Challenges of Web 2.0 and Social Media* (pp. 31–70). New York: Routledge.

Fuchs, C. (2015). *Social Media: A Critical Introduction* (1st ed.). Los Angeles: Sage.

Galinsky, A. D., & Moskowitz, G. B. (2000). Perspective-taking: Decreasing stereotype expression, stereotype accessibility, and in-group favoritism. *Journal of Personality and Social Psychology, 78* (4), pp. 708–724. doi:10.1037//0022-3514.78.4.708

Galloway, S. (2017). *The Four: The Hidden DNA of Amazon, Apple, Facebook, and Google*. New York: Penguin.

Garner, T. (2018). *Echoes of Other Worlds: Sound in Virtual Reality, Past, Present and Future*. Cham, Switzerland: Palgrave Macmillan.

Gibson, J. J. (2015). *The Ecological Approach to Visual Perception*. New York/ London: Psychology Press.

Gibson, W. (1984). *Neuromancer*. London: Ace.

Giddens, A. (1984). *The Constitution of Society*. Berkley: University of California Press.

Gilbert, G. (1980). *Photography: The Early Years*. New York: Harper & Row.

Gleasure, R., & Feller, J. (2016). A rift in the ground: Theorizing the evolution of anchor values in crowdfunding communities through the Oculus Rift case study. *Journal of the Association for Information Systems, 17* (10), pp. 708–736. doi:10.17705/ 1jais.00439

Graham, M., & Zook, M. (2011). Visualizing global cyberscapes: Mapping user-generated placemarks. *Journal of Urban Technology, 18* (1), pp. 115–132. doi:10. 1080/10630732.2011.578412

Gray, J. (2016). *The Soul of the Marionette: A Short Enquiry into Human Freedom*. London: Penguin Books.

Hardawar, D. (2018). Tobii proves that eye tracking is VR's next killer feature. *Engadget*. Retrieved March 17, 2018, from www.engadget.com/2018/01/13/ tobii-vr-eye-tracking/

Hardt, M., & Negri, A. (2000). *Empire*. Cambridge, MA: Harvard University Press.

Harman, G. (2008). DeLanda's ontology: Assemblage and realism. *Continental Philosophy Review, 41* (3), pp. 367–383. doi:10.1007/s11007-008-9084-7

Harman, G. (2010). *Towards Speculative Realism: Essays and Lectures*. Winchester: Zero Books.

Harris, B. J. (2018). *The History of the Future: How a Bunch of Misfits, Makers, and Mavericks Cracked the Code of Virtual Reality*. New York: Dey Street Books.

Hayles, N. K. (2004). Print is flat, code is deep: The importance of media-specific analysis. *Poetics Today, 25* (1), pp. 67–90. doi:10.1215/03335372-25-1-67

Hayles, N. K. (2005). *My Mother Was a Computer Digital Subjects and Literary Texts*. Chicago: University of Chicago Press.

Hayles, N. K. (2010). *How We Became Posthuman: Virtual Bodies in Cybernetics, Literature and Informatics*. Chicago: University of Chicago Press.

Hayles, N. K. (2012). *How We Think: Digital Media and Contemporary Technogenesis*. Chicago: University of Chicago Press.

Hayward, P. (1993). Situating cyberspace: The popularisation of virtual reality. In P. Hayward & T. Wollen (Eds.), *FutureVisions: New Technologies of the Screen* (pp. 180–204). London: BFI.

Heidegger, M. (1962). *Being and Time* (J. Macquarrie & E. S. Robinson, Trans.). New York: Harper.

Heidegger, M. (2008). *Basic Writings: From Being and Time (1927) to The Task of Thinking (1964)*. London: Routledge.

Heim, M. (1998). *Virtual Realism*. Oxford: Oxford University Press.

Henderson, J. (2015). Grandfather of VR: The virtual can show the beauty of the real. *NPR*. Retrieved February 01, 2018, from www.npr.org/sections/alltechconsid ered/2015/12/17/459839163/grandfather-of-vr-the-virtual-can-show-the-beauty-of-the-real

Hern, A. (2016). Oculus Rift founder Palmer Luckey spends fortune backing pro-Trump 'shitposts'. *The Guardian*. Retrieved January 09, 2018, from www.theguard ian.com/technology/2016/sep/23/oculus-rift-vr-palmer-luckey-trump-shitposts

Hillis, K. (1999). *Digital Sensations: Space, Identity, and Embodiment in Virtual Reality*. Minneapolis: University of Minnesota Press.

Hills-Duty, R. (2017). Digital catapult announce new immersive lab in brighton. *VR Focus*. Retrieved April 04, 2018, from www.vrfocus.com/2017/10/digital-catapult-announce-new-immersive-lab-in-brighton/

Holtzman, S. R. (1994). *Digital Mantras: The Languages of Abstract and Virtual Worlds*. Cambridge, MA: MIT Press.

Jarrett, K. (2016). *Feminism, Labour and Digital Media: The Digital Housewife*. New York: Routledge.

Jerald, J. (2009). *Scene-Motion- and Latency-Perception Thresholds for Head-Mounted Displays*. Master's thesis, Department of Computer Science, Chapel Hill, NC: University of North Carolina Chapel Hill.

Jerald, J. (2015). *The VR Book: Human-Centered Design for Virtual Reality*. New York: ACM.

Joffe, H., & Thompson, A. R. (2011). Thematic analysis. In D. Harper (Ed.), *Qualitative Research Methods in Mental Health and Psychotherapy Qualitative Research Methods in Mental Health and Psychotherapy: A Guide for Students and Practitioners* (pp. 210–223). New York: Wiley.

John, F. (1990). *Introduction to Communication Studies*. London: Routledge.

John, N. A. (2012). Sharing and Web 2.0: The emergence of a keyword. *New Media & Society*, *15* (2), pp. 167–182. doi:10.1177/1461444812450684

Jonnalagadda, H. (2017). Google has shipped 10 million Cardboard VR headsets since 2014. *Android Central*. Retrieved March 11, 2018, from www.androidcen tral.com/google-has-shipped-10-million-cardboard-vr-headsets-2014

Karppi, T., & Crawford, K. (2015). Social media, financial algorithms and the hack crash. *Theory, Culture & Society*, *33*(1), pp. 73–92. doi:10.1177/0263276415583139

Keen, A. (2017). The 'attention economy' created by Silicon Valley is bankrupting us. *Techcrunch*. Retrieved March 15, 2018, from https://techcrunch.com/2017/07/30/the-attention-economy-created-by-silicon-valley-is-bankrupting-us/

Keen, A. (2018). Facebook co-founder says its rise reveals the fault lines destroying the "American Dream". *Techcrunch*. Retrieved March 15, 2018, from https://

techcrunch.com/2018/03/11/facebook-co-founder-says-its-rise-reveals-the-fault-lines-destroying-the-american-dream/

Kelly, K. (2011). *What Technology Wants*. London: Penguin.

Kennedy, R. S., Lilienthal, M. G., Berbaum, K. S., Baltzley, D. R., & McCauley, M. E. (1989). Simulator sickness in U.S. Navy flight simulators. *Aviation, Space, and Environmental Medicine, 60*, pp. 10–16.

Kickstarter. (2012). *Oculus Rift: Step into the Game*. Retrieved January 07, 2018, from www.kickstarter.com/projects/1523379957/oculus-rift-step-into-the-game

Kitchin, R. (2014). *The Data Revolution: Big Data, Open Data, Data Infrastructures and Their Consequences*. Thousand Oaks, CA: Sage.

Krämer, S. (2006). The cultural techniques of time axis manipulation. *Theory, Culture & Society, 23* (7–8), pp. 93–109. doi:10.1177/0263276406069885

Lanier, J. (2010). *You Are Not a Gadget: A Manifesto*. London: Penguin.

Lanier, J. (2014). *Who Owns the Future?* London: Penguin Books.

Lanier, J. (2017). *Dawn of the New Everything: A Journey Through Virtual Reality*. London: Bodley Head.

LaValle, S. M. (2017). *Virtual Reality*. New York: Cambridge University Press. Retrieved from http://vr.cs.uiuc.edu/

Laver, K. E., George, S., Thomas, S., Deutsch, J. E., & Crotty, M. (2015). Virtual reality for stroke rehabilitation. *Cochrane Database of Systematic Reviews*. doi:10.1002/14651858.cd008349.pub3. Retrieved August 24, 2018, from https://www.cochrane.org/CD008349/STROKE_virtual-reality-stroke-rehabilitation

Lawson, B. D. (2014). Motion sickness symptomatology and origins. In K. S. Hale & K. M. Stanney (Eds.), *Handbook of Virtual Environments: Design, Implementation, and Applications* (pp. 531–599). Boca Raton, FL: CRC Press.

Lewis, P. (2018). Utterly horrifying: Ex-Facebook insider says covert data harvesting was routine. *The Guardian*. Retrieved March 20, 2018, from www.theguardian.com/news/2018/mar/20/facebook-data-cambridge-analytica-sandy-parakilas

Licklider, J. C. (1960). Man-computer symbiosis. *IRE Transactions on Human Factors in Electronics, HFE-1* (1), pp. 4–11. doi:10.1109/thfe2.1960.4503259

Lin, J. T., Wu, D., & Tao, C. (2017). So scary, yet so fun: The role of self-efficacy in enjoyment of a virtual reality horror game. *New Media & Society*. doi:10.1177/1461444817744850. Retrieved August 24, 2018, from http://journals.sagepub.com/doi/abs/10.1177/1461444817744850

Lister, M., Dovey, J., Giddings, S., Grant, I., & Kelly, K. (2003). *New Media: A Critical Introduction* (1st ed.). London: Routledge.

Lister, M., Dovey, J., Giddings, S., Grant, I., & Kelly, K. (2009). *New Media: A Critical Introduction* (2nd ed.). London: Routledge.

Lomas, N. (2017). This VR cycle is dead. *Techcrunch*. Retrieved February 01, 2018, from https://techcrunch.com/2017/08/26/this-vr-cycle-is-dead/

Lombard, M., & Ditton, T. (1997). At the heart of it all: The concept of presence. *Journal of Computer-Mediated Communication, 3* (2). doi:10.1111/j.1083–6101.1997.tb00072.x

Lovink, G. (2008). *Zero Comments: Blogging and Critical Internet Culture*. New York: Routledge.

Lovink, G. (2011). *Networks without a Cause: A Critique of Social Media*. Cambridge, MA: Polity Press.

Lovink, G. (2013). *Zero Comments: Blogging and Critical Internet Culture*. Independence: Taylor and Francis.

MacLeod, D., & Moser, M. A. (1996). *Immersed in Technology: Art and Virtual Environments*. Cambridge, MA: MIT Press.

Madsen, K. E. (2016). The differential effects of agency on fear induction using a horror-themed video game. *Computers in Human Behavior*, *56*, pp. 142–146. doi:10.1016/j.chb.2015.11.041

Magnenat-Thalmann, N., & Thalmann, D. (1994). *Artificial Life and Virtual Reality*. Chichester: Wiley.

Malpas, J. E. (2000). Uncovering the space of disclosedness: Heidegger, technology and the problem of spatiality in being and time. In H. L. Dreyfus, M. A. Wrathall, & J. E. Malpas (Eds.), *Heidegger, Authenticity, and Modernity: Essays in Honor of Hubert L. Dreyfus* (pp. 205–227). Cambridge, MA: MIT Press.

Manovich, L. (2001). *The Language of New Media*. Cambridge, MA: MIT Press.

Marx, K. (1993). *Grundrisse: Foundations of the Critique of Political Economy*. London: Penguin Books.

Matney, L. (2017). Microsoft acquires social virtual reality app AltspaceVR. *Techcrunch*. Retrieved April 14, 2018, from https://techcrunch.com/2017/10/03/microsoft-acquires-social-virtual-reality-app-altspacevr/

Matney, L. (2018). All of Oculus's Rift headsets have stopped working due to an expired certificate. *Techcrunch*. Retrieved March 08, 2018, from https://techcrunch.com/2018/03/07/all-of-oculuss-rift-headsets-have-stopped-working-due-to-an-expired-certificate/

Matney, L. (2018a). VR startup Upload shuts down its offices as funding from Palmer Luckey runs out. *Techcrunch*. Retrieved from https://techcrunch.com/2018/03/16/vr-startup-upload-shuts-down-its-offices-as-funding-from-oculus-founder-runs-out/

McGrath, J. L., Taekman, J. M., Dev, P., Danforth, D. R., Mohan, D., Kman, N., & Bond, W. F. (2017). Using virtual reality simulation environments to assess competence for emergency medicine learners. *Academic Emergency Medicine*, *25* (2), pp. 186–195. doi:10.1111/acem.13308

McLuhan, M. (1969). *Counterblast*. New York: Harcourt, Brace & World.

McLuhan, M., & McLuhan, E. (2007). *Laws of Media: The New Science*. Toronto: University of Toronto Press.

McMenemy, K., & Ferguson, S. (2007). *A Hitchhikers Guide to Virtual Reality*. Wellesley, MA: AK Peters.

Merleau-Ponty, M. (1962). *Phenomenology of Perception*. London: Routledge.

Merrin, W. (2005). *Baudrillard and the Media: A Critical Introduction*. Cambridge, MA: Polity Press.

Metz, R. (2018). Facebook's head of social VR admits there isn't much to do in its social VR app. *Technology Review*. Retrieved from www.technologyreview.com/s/611041/facebooks-head-of-social-vr-admits-there-isnt-much-to-do-in-its-social-vr-app/

Meyer, R. (2014). Everything we know about Facebook's secret mood manipulation experiment. *The Atlantic*. Retrieved March 20, 2018, from www.theatlantic.

com/technology/archive/2014/06/everything-we-know-about-facebooks-secret-mood-manipulation-experiment/373648/

Milgram, P., & Kishino, F. (1994). Taxonomy of mixed reality visual displays. *IEICE Transactions on Information and Systems, E77-D* (12), pp. 1321–1329.

Milk, C. (2015). How virtual reality can create the ultimate empathy machine. *TED Talks.* Retrieved April 01, 2018, from www.ted.com/talks/chris_milk_how_virtual_reality_can_create_the_ultimate_empathy_machine

Miller, J. (2015). The dematerializing interface. *Westminster Papers in Culture and Communication, 10* (1), pp. 66–80. doi:10.16997/wpcc.213

Mitchell, W. J. (1995). *City of Bits: Space, Place and the Infobahn.* Cambridge, MA: MIT Press.

Moore, G. E. (1965). Cramming more components onto integrated circuits. *Electronics, 38* (8), pp. 114–117.

Mori, M. (2012). The Uncanny Valley [From the Field] (K. Macdorman & N. Kageki, Trans.). *IEEE Robotics & Automation Magazine, 19* (2), pp. 98–100. doi:10.1109/mra.2012.2192811

Morozov, E. (2011). *The Net Delusion: How Not to Liberate the World.* London: Penguin.

Morozov, E. (2013). *To Save Everything, Click Here: Smart Machines, Dumb Humans and the Myth of Technological Perfectionism.* New York: Perseus Books.

Munafo, J., Diedrick, M., & Stoffregen, T. A. (2016). The virtual reality head-mounted display Oculus Rift induces motion sickness and is sexist in its effects. *Experimental Brain Research, 235* (3), pp. 889–901. doi:10.1007/s00221-016-4846-7

Nacke, L. E., Grimshaw, M. N., & Lindley, C. A. (2010). More than a feeling: Measurement of sonic user experience and psychophysiology in a first-person shooter game. *Interacting with Computers, 22* (5), pp. 336–343. doi:10.1016/j.intcom.2010.04.005

Nancy, J. (1993). *The Birth to Presence.* Stanford, CA: Stanford University Press.

Nasaw, D. (1999). *Going Out: The Rise and Fall of Public Amusements.* Cambridge, MA: Harvard University Press.

Negroponte, N. (1993). Virtual reality: Oxymoron or pleonasm? *Wired.* Retrieved February 24, 2018, from www.wired.com/1993/06/negroponte-11/

Negroponte, N. (1995). *Being Digital.* London: Coronet.

Nieborg, D. B., & Poell, T. (2018). The platformization of cultural production: Theorizing the contingent cultural commodity. *New Media & Society.* doi:10.1177/1461444818769694

Nissenbaum, H. F. (2010). *Privacy in Context: Technology, Policy, and the Integrity of Social Life.* Palo Alto, CA: Stanford University Press.

Novak, M. (1991). Liquid architectures in cyberspace. In M. Benedikt (Ed.), *Cyberspace: First Steps* (pp. 225–254). Cambridge, MA: MIT Press.

Oculus. (2012). *Update on Developer Kit Technology, Shipping Details.* Retrieved March 10, 2018, from www.oculus.com/blog/update-on-developer-kit-technology-shipping-details/

Oettermann, S. (1997). *The Panorama: History of a Mass Medium.* New York: Zone Books.

Outlaw, J. (2018). Virtual harassment: The social experience of 600 regular virtual reality (VR) users. *The Extended Mind*. Retrieved April 4, 2018, from https://extendedmind.io/blog/2018/4/4/virtual-harassment-the-social-experience-of-600-regular-virtual-reality-vrusers

Outlaw, J., & Duckles, B. (2017). Social VR. *The Extended Mind*. Retrieved October 16, 2017, from www.extendedmind.io/social-vr

Palmer, M. (2006). *Data Is the New Oil*. Retrieved March 23, 2018, from http://ana.blogs.com/maestros/2006/11/data_is_the_new.html

Parisi, D. (2016). Eine Technik der Medienberührung: Kinästhetische Displays und die Suche nach Computerhaptik. *Maske und Kothurn, 62* (2–3). doi:10.7767/muk-2016-2-310

Parisi, D. (2018). *Archaeologies of Touch: Interfacing with Haptics from Electricity to Computing*. Minneapolis: University of Minnesota Press.

Parisi, D., Paterson, M., & Archer, J. E. (2017). Haptic media studies. *New Media & Society, 19* (10), pp. 1513–1522. doi:10.1177/1461444817717518

Park, G. D., Allen, R. W., Fiorentino, D., Rosenthal, T. J., & Cook, M. L. (2006). Simulator sickness scores according to symptom susceptibility, age, and gender for an older driver assessment study. *PsycEXTRA Dataset*. doi:10.1037/e577802012-007. Retrieved August 24, 2018, from http://journals.sagepub.com/doi/abs/10.1177/154193120605002607?journalCode=proe

Paterson, M. (2007). *The Senses of Touch: Haptics, Affects and Technologies*. Oxford: Berg.

Pattenden, M. (2018). A new reality: Could VR revive the amusement arcade? *The Guardian*. Retrieved from www.theguardian.com/business/2018/may/05/vr-new-reality-revive-amusement-arcade

Pile, S., & Thrift, N. J. (1995). *Mapping the Subject: Geographies of Cultural Transformation*. London: Routledge.

Pimentel, K., & Teixeira, K. (1995). *Virtual Reality: Through the New Looking Glass*. New York: Intel/McGraw-Hill.

Pinto, D. (2017). Pornhub releases VR Porn stats, confirms most of what we knew. *TechWorm*. Retrieved March 01, 2018, from www.techworm.net/2017/05/pornhub-releases-vr-porn-stats-confirms-knew.html

Poster, M. (1995). *The Second Media Age*. Cambridge: Polity Press.

Reger, G. M., Koenen-Woods, P., Zetocha, K., Smolenski, D. J., Holloway, K. M., Rothbaum, B. O., & Gahm, G. A. (2016). Randomized controlled trial of prolonged exposure using imaginal exposure vs. virtual reality exposure in active duty soldiers with deployment-related posttraumatic stress disorder (PTSD). *Journal of Consulting and Clinical Psychology, 84* (11), pp. 946–959. doi:10.1037/ccp0000134

Rheingold, H. (1991). *Virtual Reality*. New York: Touchstone.

Riener, R., & Harders, M. (2012). *Virtual Reality in Medicine*. London: Springer.

Rimmon-Kenan, S. (2011). *Narrative Fiction: Contemporary Poetics*. London: Routledge, Taylor & Francis Group.

Riva, G. (2017). Letter to the Editor: Virtual reality in the treatment of eating and weight disorders. *Psychological Medicine, 47* (14), pp. 2567–2568. doi:10.1017/s0033291717001441

Robertson, A. (2017). Google has shipped over 10 million Cardboard VR headsets. *The Verge*. Retrieved January 30, 2018, from www.theverge.com/2017/2/28/14767902/google-cardboard-10-million-shipped-vr-ar-apps

Roettgers, J. (2018). Oculus go porn: Adult industry has high hopes for Facebook's new VR headset. *Variety*. Retrieved May 24, 2018, from https://variety.com/2018/digital/news/oculus-go-porn-adult-videos-optimized-for-go-1202820066/

Rubin, P. (2018). *Future Presence: How Virtual Reality Is Changing Human Connection, Intimacy, and the Limits of Ordinary Life*. New York: HarperOne.

Rushkoff, D. (2010). *Program or Be Programmed: Ten Commands for a Digital Age*. Berkeley, CA: Soft Skull Press.

Ryan, M. (2015). *Narrative as Virtual Reality 2: Revisiting Immersion and Interactivity in Literature and Electronic Media*. Baltimore: John Hopkins University Press.

Ryan, M. L. (2001). *Narrative as Virtual Reality: Immersion and Interactivity in Literature and Electronic Media* (1st ed.). Baltimore: Johns Hopkins University Press.

Seidel, R. J., & Chatelier, P. R. (1997). *Virtual Reality, Training's Future? Perspectives on Virtual Reality and Related Emerging Technologies*. New York: Plenum Press.

Shannon, C. E. (1948). A mathematical theory of communication. *Bell System Technical Journal, 27* (3), pp. 379–423.

Shannon, C. E., & Weaver, W. (1999). *The Mathematical Theory of Communication*. Urbana: University of Illinois Press.

Shelstad, W. J., Smith, D. C., & Chaparro, B. S. (2017). Gaming on the rift: How virtual reality affects game user satisfaction. *Proceedings of the Human Factors and Ergonomics Society Annual Meeting, 61* (1), pp. 2072–2076. doi:10.1177/1541931213602001

Sher, W., Williams, A., Gameson, R., & Sherratt, S. (2012). Changing skills in changing environments: Skills needed in virtual construction teams. In C. S. Lanyi (Ed.), *Applications of Virtual Reality* (pp. 31–49). Rijeka, Croatia: INTECH Open Access Publisher.

Sheridan, T. B. (1992). Musings on telepresence and virtual presence. *Presence: Teleoperators and Virtual Environments, 1* (1), pp. 120–126. doi:10.1162/pres.1992.1.1.120

Sherman, W. R., & Craig, A. B. (2002). *Understanding Virtual Reality: Interface, Application and Design*. San Francisco: Morgan Kaufmann.

Shields, R. (2003). *The Virtual*. New York: Routledge.

Simandan, D. (2010). Beware of contingency. *Environment and Planning D: Society and Space, 28* (3), pp. 388–396. doi:10.1068/d2310

Sirius, R. (2007). *Whatever Happened to Virtual Reality?* Retrieved January 09, 2018, from www.10zenmonkeys.com/2007/03/09/whatever-happened-to-virtual-reality/

Slater, M. (2009). Place illusion and plausibility can lead to realistic behaviour in immersive virtual environments. *Philosophical Transactions of the Royal Society B: Biological Sciences, 364* (1535), pp. 3549–3557.

Slater, M., & Wilbur, S. (1997). A Framework for Immersive Virtual Environments (FIVE): Speculations on the role of presence in virtual environments. *Presence: Teleoperators and Virtual Environments, 6* (6), pp. 603–616. doi:10.1162/pres.1997.6.6.603

Smythe, D. (2001). On the audience commodity and its work. In M. G. Durham & D. Kellner (Eds.), *Media and Cultural Studies: Keyworks* (pp. 230–256). Malden, MA: Blackwell.

Snow, B. (2007). The 10 worst-selling consoles of all time. *GamePro*. Retrieved January 30, 2018, from www.gamepro.com/gamepro/domestic/games/features/111823.shtml

Solon, O. (2018). Tim Berners-Lee: We must regulate tech firms to prevent weaponised web. *The Guardian*. Retrieved March 11, 2018, from www.theguardian.com/technology/2018/mar/11/tim-berners-lee-tech-companies-regulations

Srnicek, N. (2016). *Platform Capitalism*. Cambridge, UK: Polity Press.

Stam, R., Burgoyne, R., & Flitterman-Lewis, S. (1992). *New Vocabularies in Film Semiotics: Structuralism, Post-Structuralism and Beyond*. London: Routledge.

Stanyer, J. (2009). Web 2.0 and the transformation of news and journalism. In A. Chadwick & P. N. Howard (Eds.), *Routledge Handbook of Internet Politics* (pp. 201–213). New York: Routledge.

Steinicke, F. (2016). *Being Really Virtual: Immersive Natives and the Future of Virtual Reality*. New York: Springer Berlin Heidelberg.

Stephenson, N. (1992). *Snow Crash*. New York: Bantam Books.

Strain, E. (1999). Virtual VR. *Convergence: The International Journal of Research into New Media Technologies*, *5*(2), pp. 10–15. doi:10.1177/135485659900500202

Sutherland, I. E. (1963). *Sketchpad: A Man-Machine Graphical Communication System*. Unpublished Master's thesis, Massachusetts Institute of Technology, Cambridge, MA.

Sutherland, I. E. (1968). A head-mounted three dimensional display. *Proceedings of the December 9–11, 1968, Fall Joint Computer Conference, part I on—AFIPS 68 (Fall, part I)*. doi:10.1145/1476589.1476686. Retrieved August 24, 2018, frin https://dl.acm.org/citation.cfm?id=1476686

Tamborini, R., & Skalski, P. (2006). The role of presence in the experience of electronic games. In J. Bryant & P. Vorderer (Eds.), *Playing Video Games: Motives, Responses, and Consequences* (pp. 225–240). New York: Routledge.

Taplin, J. (2017). *Move Fast and Break Things: How Facebook, Google, and Amazon Have Cornered Culture and What It Means for All of Us*. London: Macmillan.

Terranova, T. (2004). *Network Culture: Politics for the Information Age*. London: Pluto Press.

Thon, J. (2008). Immersion revisited. On the value of a contested concept. In O. Leino, H. Wirman, & A. Fernandez (Eds.), *Extending Experiences: Structure, Analysis and Design of Computer Game Player Experience* (pp. 29–43). Rovaniemi: Lapland University Press.

Thrift, N. (2008). Pass it on: Towards a political economy of propensity. *Emotion, Space and Society*, *1* (2), pp. 83–96. doi:10.1016/j.emospa.2009.02.004

Tinnell, J. (2018). Is virtual reality undemocratic? *The Boston Review*. Retrieved March 15, 2018, from http://bostonreview.net/science-nature/john-tinnell-is-virtual-reality-undemocratic

Torres, J. (2018). Lenovo Mirage Solo with Daydream hands-on: VR and the camera to shoot it. *Slashgear*. Retrieved January 09, 2018, from www.slashgear.com/lenovo-mirage-solo-with-daydream-hands-on-vr-and-the-camera-to-shoot-it-09514126/

Turkle, S. (2011). *Alone Together: Why We Expect More from Technology and Less from Each Other*. New York: Basic Books.

Urban Dictionary. (n.d.). *Shit Posting*. Retrieved January 09, 2018, from www.urbandictionary.com/define.php?term=Shit Posting

Van Dijck, J. (2013). *The Culture of Connectivity: A Critical History of Social Media*. New York: Oxford University Press.

Virilio, P. (2008). *Open Sky*. London: Verso.

Virtual Reality Society. (2017). *VPL Research Jaron Lanier*. Retrieved January 30, 2018, from www.vrs.org.uk/virtual-reality-profiles/vpl-research.html

Walsh, J. (1995). Virtual reality: Almost here, almost there, nowhere yet. *Convergence, 1* (1).

Walton, M. (2016). Eyes of the Animal lets you become a bat—in VR. *Arstechnica*. Retrieved January 13, 2018, from https://arstechnica.com/gaming/2016/07/laser-feast-eyes-of-the-animal-vr/

Watercutter, A. (2018). Virtual reality takes a political turn in the trump era. *Wired*. Retrieved May 21, 2018, from www.wired.com/story/tribeca-film-festival-vr-political

Welch, C. (2014). Facebook buying Oculus VR for $2 billion. *The Verge*. Retrieved January 07, 2018, from www.theverge.com/2014/3/25/5547456/facebook-buying-oculus-for-2-billion/in/3631187

Welling, W. (1987). *Photography in America: The Formative Years, 1839–1900*. Albuquerque: University of New Mexico.

Westwood, J. D., Westwood, S. W., & Felländer-Tsai, L. (2016). *Medicine Meets Virtual Reality 22: NextMed /MMVR22*. Amsterdam: IOS Press.

Whyte, J., & Nikolic, D. (2018). *Virtual Reality and the Built Environment*. London: Routledge.

Wiener, N. (1954). *The Human Use of Human Beings: Cybernetics and Society*. New York: Da Capo Press.

Wiener, N. (2016). *Cybernetics: Or, Control and Communication in the Animal and the Machine*. New York: Quid Pro Books.

Williams, R. (1974). *Television: Technology and Cultural Form*. London: Collins.

Wood, M., Wood, G., & Balaam, M. (2017). 'They're just tixel pits, man': Disputing the 'reality' of virtual reality pornography through the story completion method. *Proceedings of the 2017 CHI Conference on Human Factors in Computing Systems—CHI 17*. doi:10.1145/3025453.3025762. Retrieved August 24, 2018, from https://www.researchgate.net/publication/316709117_They%27re_Just_Tixel_Pits_Man_Disputing_the_%27Reality%27_of_Virtual_Reality_Pornography_through_the_Story_Completion_Method

Woodard, J. W. (1934). Critical notes on the culture lag concept. *Social Forces, 12* (3), 388–398. doi:10.2307/2569930

Woolley, B. (1992). *Virtual Worlds: A Journey in Hype and Hyperreality*. Harmondsworth: Penguin Books.

Wu, T. (2017). *The Attention Merchants: From the Daily Newspaper to Social Media, How Our Time and Attention is Harvested and Sold*. London: Atlantic Books.

Index

For Product Safety Concerns and Information please contact our EU
representative GPSR@taylorandfrancis.com Taylor & Francis Verlag GmbH,
Kaufingerstraße 24, 80331 München, Germany

Batch number: 08153772

Printed by Printforce, the Netherlands